RESEARCH ON EDUCATIONAL INNOVATIONS

Arthur Ellis and Jeffrey Fouts

Eye On Education
P.O. Box 388
Princeton Junction, NJ 08550
(609) 799-9188
(609) 799-3698 fax

The authors would like to acknowledge the work of Shirley Riley who helped assemble the research for this book.

For information about permission to reproduce selections from this book, write:
Eye On Education, Permissions Dept., Box 388, Princeton Junction, NJ 08550

Library of Congress Catalog Card Number: 93-70822

ISBN 1-883001-05-6

Printed in the United States of America

Printing 9 8 7 6 5 4

PREFACE

Enlighten me now, O Muses,
    tenants of Olympian homes,
For you are goddesses, inside
    on everything, knowing everything.
But we mortals hear only the
    new, and know nothing at all.

Homer

Welcome to this book. It is about educational innovation. We are fascinated by the new: new cars, new fashions, new insights, etc. There is something exciting and motivating about newness. Think about it: new hope, new beginnings. In recent American political history we have had both the New Deal and the New Frontier. Our desire to try something new is often based on a wish to break with the past and the present, especially where feelings of discontent exist.

American schools have become seedbeds of discontent in recent times. Everywhere we read about the loss of confidence in our schools on the part of the public. Anyone who follows the story line has heard talk of a golden era in American public education. Our current efforts are placed alongside those of a mythical past and found wanting. And even for those who don't spend a lot of time longing for the school days of yesteryear, there is always the desire to improve, to do better. We set our goals not at levels of mediocracy, but at the far reaches of excellence.

So the search for what is new and good continues. The

dream of every teacher and administrator is of new heights of achievement, civic participation, and personal fulfilment for the next generation. Much hope exists for the young. We see that hope at the PTA meeting when so many parents of kindergarten and first grade children show up. And we see the hope turn to reality, for better or for worse, as children find their way through the school years.

Like pilgrims in quest of the Holy Grail, we look for the curriculum or method that will get us where we want to go, to the land of excellence. And with great perseverance and unflagging good cheer, we are willing to try this or that innovation, hoping that at last we have something better than we've ever had before. We hear about cooperative learning, and we agree to try it because maybe it will improve the social fabric of classroom life and raise achievement at the same time. We learn about outcome-based education and wonder why we didn't think to make our learning outcomes clear all along. And we read an article on brain-based learning and find ourselves agreeing that, of course, the little 3-pound organ called the human brain has unlimited capabilities.

So the quest continues. Each year, it seems, new ideas about improving the system are brought to our attention, sometimes with great fanfare. Some of them literally scream for our attention bringing to mind the centuries-old words of the writer Baltasar Gracian, who noted that a brand new mediocrity is thought more of than accustomed excellence.

One of the things we wish to accomplish in this book is to help you separate the "brand new mediocrities" from that which is excellent, whether old or new. To do this we had to set up a screen, much in the way someone panning for gold in a mountain stream uses a screen or pan to dip into the rushing waters. The screen allows that which is not valuable to return to the creek while the rich ore is retained. It's not a perfect system whether you are seeking gold ore or golden educational ideas. But if you are persistent, and we were, you will find some nuggets.

Our screen is published research. We use it for two reasons. The first is that everyone has access to published research through the readily available journals in education.

This is not true of unpublished research. It is often nearly impossible to access. Much of the time we know about it only because someone touting an innovation refers to certain glowing results without showing us the conditions, the controls, the design, and the analysis.

The second reason for our setting this standard is that published research has undergone levels of careful scrutiny that unpublished research never experiences. Does this mean that unpublished research is necessarily bad? We think not, but we can tell you that we have carefully examined much unpublished research. Most of the time it simply does not meet the standards that you would knowingly demand if you were about to spend much time, energy, and money on a particular innovation. Research published in such journals as the *Journal of Educational Research* or the *Journal of Educational Psychology* is carefully reviewed by knowledgeable jurors prior to acceptance, or in most cases, prior to rejection. In other words, you never even see the faulty research because it doesn't appear in these journals.

We are excited about educational innovation, just as we hope you are. But there is no point in becoming excited about so-called improvements that really give us no proof of their goodness. Nothing is gained in the name of innovation when we find ourselves in the very same circumstance as that of the ancient Roman general Pyrrhus, who said "One more such victory and we are undone." Our role is that of messengers, and we are fully aware that in ancient times messengers were often thrown into a well when they brought bad tidings, and merely taken for granted when the news they brought was good. We accept this in good humor. So be prepared: Some of the tidings we bring are good and some are less than that.

Let us all agree that we seek progress and not merely change. We respect your judgment, and it is in that spirit that we bring this information about educational innovations to you. We ask only that you review our findings as well as those of others and reach your own conclusions. It was observed long ago that one's judgment is only as good as one's information, and our goal is to inform you.

About the Authors

Arthur Ellis is Professor of Education at Seattle Pacific University. Previously, he taught in public schools and at the University of Minnesota. He is the author of eight published books and numerous journal articles. He consults to the National Science Foundation and to various school systems in the United States and abroad.

Jeffrey Fouts is Professor of Education at Seattle Pacific University. Previously, he taught in public schools in the State of Oregon. He is the author of two published books and has done research on classroom environments as well as consulting work in the United States and in other countries.

CONTENTS

CONTENTS

CONTENTS

CONTENTS

CHAPTER ONE

THE NATURE OF EDUCATIONAL INNOVATION

"One doesn't discover new lands without consenting to lose sight of the shore for a very long time."

Andre Gide

Each generation must answer anew a set of age-old questions. Those questions go to the heart of our existence. They are questions of purpose, of being, of destiny. They are questions of justice, of relationships, of goodness. The fact that previous generations have grappled with the same questions is not the point. The questions are so basic that we must address them; we ignore them at our peril. Others cannot answer them for us, although they can give us insights. We must seek our own answers, however different or similar to those arrived at by our predecessors. This is so because the search is as important as the outcome. It is the process of arriving at answers, however tentative or even deficient, that makes us human.

Just as we seek answers to life's larger questions, we seek answers within the frames of our professional existence, in this case teaching and learning. As teachers and administrators, we seek answers to questions about the nature of knowledge, the nature of learning, the nature of teaching. We ask ourselves if there is a better way to organize instruction, a better way to present ideas to young people, a better way to assess learning.

We grapple with such dualism as control vs. freedom, cooperation vs. independence, time-on-task vs. creativity. As practical people working in school settings, with all the complexities one finds in such socially contrived environments as playgrounds and lunchrooms, and such academically contrived environments as high school physics classes and primary reading classes, we wonder what to teach, how to teach it, and even if what we teach has lasting value. These questions tend to deplete one's resources, especially when we read in the popular press that American schools are doing a poor job of preparing the nation's young for an increasingly complex future.

At the same time, the educational literature is filled with ideas and strategies for innovation: Outcome-based education; whole language learning; interdisciplinary curriculum; learning styles; developmentally-appropriate practice; cooperative learning; effective teaching; school restructuring; site-based management; and the list goes on. Each of these innovations is touted by its proponents as the key to an improved school life for teachers and students. Administrators read about a given innovation and wonder whether it could be the answer for their school. Like wandering nomads in search of the next oasis, we move from fad to fad in search of the next wellspring with the vague hope that we might find a permanent place to settle. But, of course, we never do.

What is the source of our ambivalence toward innovation in education? On the one hand, we seem ready, as educational historian Herbert Kleibard has pointed out, to grasp at anything so long as it is *new*. None of us wants our school to be left behind. On the other hand, those teachers and administrators who have been around for awhile have seen so many things come and go in the name of innovation that a certain degree of cynicism sets in when they are told at the fall faculty meeting that "we are going to become an 'effective school,'" or whatever.

In this book we have attempted to provide teachers, administrators, and other school personnel with insights to a carefully selected set of innovations. The innovations chosen to appear in these pages have nationwide, if not international, impact and applicability across a range of grade and subject levels, and considerable staying power. As you read about them, you should gain insights not only to certain specific innovations, but insights to the nature of innovation itself and how one might ask oneself to what extent a particular innovation, perhaps one that is yet to appear, is not merely new, but worthwhile.

At this point a cautionary note must be sounded. No new idea, no matter how well researched, is worthwhile outside a context of purpose. For example, if we were asked "Is an interdisciplinary curriculum a good idea for my school?," we would be forced to respond by asking "What is the purpose of your school?" No one can answer that question meaningfully except the people who have a genuine interest in your school. Now this may seem rather simplistic and even obvious to everyone. But the history of failure and disappointment in educational innovation starts with confusion of purpose. It inevitably leads to cynicism and the "we tried that" syndrome.

So somewhere in the matrix of your individual and school goal structure you must take the measure of any new educational idea. The more meaningful question is not "Is it good?" but "Is it good for us?" Each educator and each school faculty must face the same basic questions:

- What does our school stand for?
- What should students learn?
- What are the best conditions for learning?
- What teacher behavior enhances learning?
- How should classes and schools be organized?

. . . and so on. The questions are endless because:

- Teaching is as much an art as a science.
- Students are diverse and they respond differentially.
- Societal needs and demands change.

• Local and site-specific needs differ considerably.

WHERE ARE THEY NOW?

A generation ago a series of innovations entered the world of education. Depending on your age and/or your powers of recollection, you may recognize some of them. They included career education, values clarification, multicultural education, human relations training, open schools, competency-based education, peace education, back to the basics, bilingual education, and a few others. Where are they now? The answers vary. Some disappeared without a trace. Some are the forerunners of present-day reform efforts. Some are still around in one form or another. This will always be the case. Today's trend is often tomorrow's forgotten dream. Some of the innovations that sweep through the school scene are nothing more than fads. Some have greater staying power. Let's look at why this might be so.

RESEARCH BASED?

A common claim of most educational innovations is that they are "research-based." The intent, apparently, is to give school personnel cause to think that a particular program is valid and reasonable for them to use. The term "research-based" lends almost mystical qualities to the innovation, making it difficult if not impossible for the average teacher, administrator, or school board member to challenge the claims made in behalf of the innovation. Who among us, after all, is going to challenge RESEARCH? The fact is that many school personnel simply do not understand the arcane language of educational research with its language of statistical analysis, control groups, experimental designs, etc. As a result, they are left to the mercy of persuasive arguments by "experts" who tell them what to do. We will try to demystify the process.

To begin it is useful to consider examples of research from the field of natural science because science has served as the paradigm for most social science research of which educational research is a subset. We begin with the idea of theory. Theories are *tentative* ways of explaining and predicting observed phenomena. The development of a theoretical model is the quest of persons doing pure or basic scientific research. While working in the field of physics, Albert Einstein developed his theory of relativity, a theory that stated that all motion must be defined relative to a frame of reference. In other words, space and time are relative, not absolute, concepts. They take on meaning in relation to their context. Einstein proposed his ideas as a theoretical model, not as a fact. Other physicists have conducted research on the theory, finding much supportive evidence for it. Today the theory of relativity serves as a useful model for the explanation and prediction of the behavior of matter and energy. However, as a theory it is subject to new interpretation, and in time it may well be modified considerably in the light of new knowledge.

Most often, scientific theory emerges as the result of some preliminary research in a particular field. When Charles Darwin sailed aboard *H.M.S. Beagle* to the Galapagos Islands and to the South Pacific in the 19th Century he made careful, systematic, observations of certain animals and their unique characteristics. From his collected data he advanced a hypothesis that changes in the physical characteristics of animals were the result of an ongoing, evolutionary process. More than a century later, his theory of evolution remains the object of scientific study although it has itself evolved considerably over time. Many questions have been answered, but far more questions remain so research on the topic continues.

Our first two examples are about the behavior of matter and energy and adaptive change in the physical characteristics of animals. As complex as those issues are (we don't pretend to understand them except at a rudimentary level), they seem pure and uncomplicated when compared to theories advanced within the frame of the social sciences. The theories of Sigmund Freud and Karl Marx, for example, were social theories. Freud developed a theory of personality based on research with his patients who were mainly institutionalized sexually abused women. In time, he built a huge amount of scaffolding around his observations. His ideas became so pervasive that, as a result of his work, whole terminologies entered the vocabulary of the middle class (for example, "Freudian slip"). His ideas seemed more like facts than theories to most people. Today his ideas seem rather quaint, and unlike Darwin's or Einstein's, are not really the basis for advancements in the field of psychological research.

The theories of Karl Marx were tried out on about half the world's population under the name "Communism." Marx theorized a leadership of the working class and a utopian society unfettered by religion, private ownership, and other traditional forms of thought and practice. One might argue whether Marx's pure theory was in fact what was institutionalized in the former USSR, China, etc., but there would be few takers in Russia, Poland, or Hungary today given the opportunity to try it again in improved form. As bizarre and ugly as the socialist "experiment" called Marxism has been, it does serve to make a point to consumers of educational research: Theories of human behavior have real, lasting consequences when we try them out on human beings. So we had better be careful when we even consider applying them to our classrooms and schools. The leap from theory to practice is often a distant leap and one fraught with imminent peril.

HOW EDUCATIONAL THEORIES DEVELOP

Basic or pure research findings are often used to develop theoretical models of learning. Those theoretical models are then used to derive implications for education. The educational implications are in turn packaged as a coherent set of teaching strategies, learner activities, and classroom/school structural changes. In other words, the packagers suggest, change what you are doing presently to their new approach. Why? Because it is better and the "research" shows that to be true or we would not ask you to do it.

Notice that three steps are involved along the way to your classroom or school: (1) pure research; (2) educational implications; and (3) suggested classroom/school practice. Let's examine the steps one at a time using a specific example, *cooperative learning.*

Level One

In the 1940's and 1950's, a social psychologist named Morton Deutsch used his research findings to develop a theory of social interdependence. Like most good scientific researchers, Deutsch was familiar with prior research, especially, in this case, the work of Kurt Lewin in the 1930's. Lewin had developed an idea called field theory which said in essence that a group was actually a "dynamic whole" rather than a mere collection of individuals. What Lewin meant is that the behavior of members in a group is interactive, thereby creating the potential for greater outcomes than one might get merely by adding the sum of the parts of a group. "Deutsch theorized that social interdependence exists only when the goals of individuals in a group are affected, for better or worse, by the others." It was the "better" that intrigued him. Using Lewin's idea that the whole is greater than the sum of its parts, Deutsch felt that when people with common goals worked with each other in cooperative fashion something better happened than when they either worked alone or competed with each other. Deutsch went on to theorize that the process is enhanced when individuals *perceive* that they can reach their goals only if other members of their group can also reach their goals. In repeated experiments, Deutsch found that his theory seemed to hold up. He published his results thus allowing others to support, extend, or challenge his findings in the free marketplace of intellectual endeavor.

Level Two

In time educational researchers began to show interest in the theory of social interdependence. They reasoned that what worked in small groups and workplace settings where the theory had originally been field tested might also work in classrooms. School classrooms seemed like a logical place to apply the theory of social interdependence since a typical room has about 30 kids who traditionally each work alone, or who, even when placed in groups, may not have the skills to identify and achieve a common goal. Also, because of tradition, etc., most students probably do not perceive that they can better attain their academic goals if other students improve as well. The research studies in classrooms, of which there have been many, were driven by questions of increased achievement, increased motivation to learn, attitude toward school, attitude toward fellow students, and other outcomes. Among the leading level two researchers are Robert Slavin and David and Roger Johnson. As the efficacy of cooperative learning became clear, especially its beneficial effects in conceptual and problem solving tasks, the push for teachers and administrators to use it in classrooms became overwhelming.

Level Three

Efficacious outcomes for cooperative learning were increasingly reported at professional meetings and in research in education journals throughout the 1970's and 1980's. Many of the reported studies had been conducted in school class rooms across a range of grade and subject matter levels. It was at this point that workshops, sometimes held by the researchers themselves, began to spring up around the country. Any teacher or administrator interested in applying cooperative learning in the classroom or school had little trouble finding workshops, institutes, retreats, classes, or "practical" articles in such magazines as *Instructor*, *Learning*, etc. In short, cooperative learning was sweeping through the educational community like wildfire. The workshops, etc., were focused on practical applications of the theory. Teachers wanted answers to such questions as "How do I know the slower students won't just copy the ideas of better students?" and "How do I measure individual achievement?" and "What do I do if a kid won't cooperate with other members of the group?" and "How is this different from just assigning kids to committees?" Out of these excellent, practical questions came new educational research studies and new books, such as *Leading the Cooperative School* (1989), by David and Roger Johnson.

Thus more than 50 years after the theory of social inter-dependence began to crystallize, the ongoing refinement of school and classroom applications of cooperative learning continues. At this point, more than 300 research studies conducted in classroom settings and school districts are avail-able. Literally thousands of policy articles can be found on the topic. And all of this is completely necessary simply because it's a long leap from a theory of social interdependence formulated by social psychologists in the 1930's to a third grade science class near the turn of the 21st Century.

We selected cooperative learning as a case study in the nature of educational innovation because it strikes us as a positive example of the gradual unfolding of the process of how a theory germinates and how it ultimately finds its way to classroom practice. And notice how, if the theory has real promise, it will interact with classroom practice in such a way as to cause further refinement of the theory. Thus the process is cyclical rather than linear. If it were linear, we would simply impose the finished product on a classroom. This has been done, as you probably know, with disastrous consequences. The exciting aspect of the teacher's role or that of the admin-istrator is that they can be a fundamental part of the process. This is so not because they say an idea is good or no good, but because they are the keys to the ongoing refinement of an idea. The practical application of ideas by teachers and students in real-world educational settings represents the best test of an idea's staying power.

CONCLUSION

Each of the 10 educational innovations that we will examine in this book began as a theory far removed from classroom life. Each ultimately found its way into the classrooms and schools of America. We propose to examine how that happened. Our analysis of each will raise a basic set of questions. Those questions include:

• How good was the original theory on which the idea is based?

- How appropriate is the research that advocates the use of this theory in school settings?

- What does this theory purport to do that will improve life in schools and classrooms?

- What claims are made in behalf of the theory as a necessary component of the school curriculum?

- What are the requisite conditions of the theory for school success?

- Why would someone want to use this theory in school settings?

Classroom life unfolds within a complex set of conditions. The list of human and material variables is endless. No two classrooms are the same, just as no two communities are the same. The mere addition or subtraction of one student in a classroom changes the circumstances. Each teacher's personal, practical sense of teaching and learning is different. The leadership is variable from one school to the next ranging from dynamic to nil. The public's perception of schools in each community has much to do with a school's success or failure. And, of course, what happens in families matters even more than what happens at school.

As teachers and administrators we are always trying to improve ourselves. We want our efforts to help young people to learn to be productive. Therefore we seek the help of others who also care and who can help us. And that is what this book is about.

CHAPTER TWO

THE STRUCTURE OF EDUCATIONAL INNOVATION

"Out of every ten innovations attempted, all very splendid, nine will end up in silliness."

Antonio Machado

It can be argued that there is very little that is new in education. It can be argued, and has been, that there is nothing new under the sun. Most things have been tried before in some form. But our experiences are different from those of the previous generation because they are *our* experiences. As we consider the many problems of teaching and learning, new perspectives (at least they're new to us) emerge and compete for our attention. In these times of sustained criticism of the educational system, new ideas, new terminology, and new reform programs are abundant simply because people sincerely want to improve things. In fact, the proliferation of new programs, which range from the well-researched to something less than that, has reached a level of staggering proportions.

At this point it will serve us well to return to some of the ideas presented in Chapter One. The chart presented in Figure 2.1 illustrates how innovative programs are developed. Early in the movement someone identifies some research which suggests a theory about learning. The theory might emerge from insight into human behavior, thinking processes, or percep-

Figure 2.1. The Development of Innovative Programs

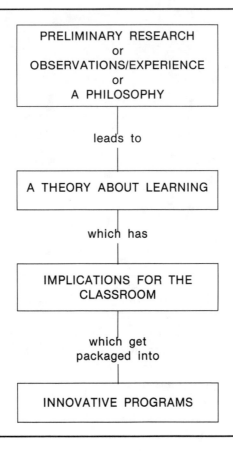

tions of reality, just to name a few examples. In any event the theory of learning may have implications for how teachers should teach and under what type of conditions students learn best. Jean Piaget's theory of development of the intellect, for example, clearly identified age-related stages through which one progresses. Further, the theory stated that persons in a particular stage of development are capable of certain intellectual activities and not capable of some others which must happen later. This theory intrigued a number of educational researchers who wished to apply Piaget's ideas to school settings, something Piaget himself had never done. Some researchers hypothesized that intellectual development could be accelerated with enriched programs. But to the best of our knowledge, this idea does not have anything close to sufficient empirical support. Piaget was amused by this line of thinking; he called it the "American question."

In any event, at some point someone in the education field thinks through the implications of a given theory and packages the ideas into a delivery system suitable for use in educational settings. The system might be designed to change teacher behavior, student behavior, or classroom environments to conform to the ideal set of conditions on which the theory is predicated.

REAPING THE WHIRLWIND

What is the role of educational research in all of this? And how is educational research different from systematic program evaluation? The claims are that many of these innovative programs are researched-based. We must point out that there is a difference between saying that a program is research-based, and that research has shown a program to be effective under certain conditions. Unfortunately, many educators do not make this crucial distinction. *In fact, the best that many of the innovations can claim is that the theory and resulting programs are developed from basic research, often in psychology, into programs for teaching and learning. Other programs are based on unproven theoretical models only, with scant research to support the theory.* This is the realm of question posing that educators should enter with those who tout a particular program.

Ideally, before thousands or millions of dollars are spent on educational changes, *programs* should be subjected to careful, unbiased investigation through the evaluation of pilot programs. Unfortunately, as educational researcher Robert Slavin has pointed out, this generally tends to happen *toward the end* of the cycle of the innovation, after the rush has died down, and districts have moved on to some other new staff development activity or program. Thus, we reap the whirl-wind.

How did our profession get caught up in this succession of fad-driven spirals of innovation based not on goodness, but on newness? Slavin (1989), one of the most active researchers in the educational community, has observed and examined this phenomenon over the years. His insights into the process are rather revealing. He writes that "generational progress does occur in education, but it is usually a product of changes in society, rather than changes in educational techniques themselves. For example, the clearly beneficial trend toward desegregation and more equal treatment of minorities represents true generational progress, but it arose from social and legal changes, not from educational innovation. More often, education resembles such fields as fashion and design, in which change mirrors shifts in taste and social climate, and is not usually thought of as true progress" (p. 752).

Slavin further states that "one of the most important reasons for the continuing existence of the educational pendulum is that educators rarely wait for or demand hard evidence before adopting new practices on a wide scale. Of course, every innovator claims research support for his or her methods; at a minimum, there is usually a 'gee whiz' story or two about a school or district that was 'turned around' by the innovation. Alternatively, a developer may claim that, while the program itself has not been formally evaluated, the principles on which it is based are supported by research" (p. 753).

THE HUNTER MODEL: "ONE MORE SUCH VICTORY AND WE ARE UNDONE."

The Roman General Pyrrhus gives us the term "Pyrrhic Victory," an allusion to his many battlefield triumphs accompanied by horrendous casualties among his own troops. There are many such "victories" in the annals of education, but here is a recent example. Slavin examines in detail the Madeline Hunter model. He calls Hunter "perhaps the most popular educational trainer of our time" (p. 754). We have not included a chapter on

Hunter in this book because the movement itself appears to be fading fast. But it can serve as an excellent example of what happens in the name of educational innovation.

Since it seems almost inconceivable that there are educators today who have not heard of the Hunter program or model, we will give it only the briefest overview here. The model is sometimes called Instructional Theory Into Practice (ITIP) or Program for Effective Teaching (PET). It emerged in the early 1970's with a series of books and workshops by Madeline Hunter. Throughout the 1970's and well into the 1980's, schools, and oftentimes entire districts and states, provided inservice training in the Hunter model. Entire staff development programs and faculty evaluation procedures were based on it. District personnel officers would routinely quiz prospective teachers on their knowledge of the Hunter model. Courses for preservice and inservice teachers, where people actually got college credit for studying ITIP "theory," were offered throughout the land. Student teachers were expected to develop lesson plans and units that used the ITIP steps to effective teaching as a template. Teachers themselves were often divided over the program. Many became advocates and some were trained as trainers themselves in ITIP. Others shrugged it off as one more fad they had to endure. A few brave souls openly questioned the validity of the entire thing, but that took a lot of courage. The amazing thing is that as it disappears, there are no apologies, seemingly no regrets. But the lesson to be learned is enormous. It draws out the danger present in what the philosopher Francis Bacon called "The Idol of the Tribe." When the Idol of the Tribe is being worshiped, no one dares question the process because, after all, everyone is doing it. It's the "in" thing to do.

The ITIP or PET program itself is a method for analyzing the key elements of a lesson with suggested procedures for lesson development. It was purportedly based on educational and psychological theory and research. It focused on four elements: (1) Teaching to an objective (generally a behavioral objective); (2) teaching at the correct level of (cognitive) difficulty; (3) monitoring and adjusting instruction (*i.e.*, formative evaluation and re-teaching, mastery learning); and (4) using the principles of learning (*e.g.*, reinforcement theories, motivational theories, etc.).

The ITIP movement followed the "pendulum" swing described by Slavin. It serves as a classic example. The program was proposed in the early 1970's and implemented in a few school districts. Claims of great success were made. The word spread rapidly that here at last was a research-based program that worked in real-world school settings. ITIP became "derigueur" among staff developers. By the late 1970's and early 1980's the movement had begun to sweep the country even though there were no quality studies that showed the program was at all effective in increasing student learning. Complaints by researchers were either ignored or thought of as sour grapes. Anecdotal stories served to verify the program's success.

The program's originator, Madeline Hunter, appeared at conventions, wrote articles, and consulted to school districts directly. Where she was unavailable, surrogates took her place. At its peak, the Hunter program was being used, and in many cases enforced by district officers, in all 50 states. Its popularity exceeded any phenomenon in modern school practice history.

By the mid-to-late 1980's interest in the program began to wane as staff developers moved on to other topics such as learning styles and outcome-based education. They did this not because the latter were proven to be any better but because they became the latest fad. About this time evaluation results of ITIP programs showed that the program had no more positive impact on student learning than random efforts by teachers. The research results mattered little because by the time they weighed in, ITIP had pretty much run its course. New fads had taken its place.

IN RETROSPECT

What was touted as an educational program based on "research" was actually a classic example of the process of implementation we described earlier. Many of the elements of ITIP *were* based on psychological *research* and *learning theory*. But the implementation of the program itself had not been evaluated with quality research to determine its effectiveness in increasing student learning. For example, reinforcement was identified as one of the key components of ITIP. Psychological research has, in fact, clearly shown that positive reinforcement of learning predictably results in increased learning. Similarly, psychological research has also shown that the immediacy of feedback, another ITIP protocol, can serve as a motivating factor in learning. Both of these are elements of ITIP that have a substantiated research base. Other elements of ITIP, such as the correct level of difficulty, were based on theoretical models, in this instance, Benjamin Bloom's taxonomy of educational objectives in the cognitive domain, a model the very vocabulary of which raises fundamental questions.

In this manner, then, ITIP was presented as a research-based model of teaching and learning. And in one sense it was. Certain individual elements were based on psychological research in the area of learning. In other words, specific elements of the program may have been sound in and of themselves under given conditions. But when the entire package was put together as a unified model, that is, when individual research findings and theories were combined to form one large model, it was no longer appropriate to say that ITIP was research-based. The very act of conceptualizing ITIP resulted in a new construct consisting of many divergent research findings and theories, a new entity that had not been researched at all. And in retrospect, that may be giving ITIP too much credit. Actually, the German educator Johann Herbart had conceptualized an almost identical scheme in the 19th Century, one that identified five points in effective teaching. It, too, swept across our landscape like a prairie fire! Today, only a handful of educators has even heard of it, much less know much about it.

Perhaps an analogy will serve us well in an attempt to explain this complex issue. We know from the laws of physics that a billiard ball struck at a certain angle by another moving billiard ball will behave in predictable fashion, at least on a flat, well-made felt covered billiard table where there is no competing, interfering variable, such as gale-force winds, the table propped at a 45 degree angle, molasses poured on the surface, etc. But what happens to our billiard ball, even under optimum conditions, if the table is littered with a dozen other billiard balls? The answer is that the laws of physics still work, but the situation is quite complex because of the probable interaction of the other balls with the ball that is initially struck. So now we have balls going in all kinds of directions. Actually, a billiard table littered with billiard balls is a fairly simple situation compared to a classroom filled with 30 students. Thus, a theory about motivation developed under controlled conditions during a psychological experiment has only limited predictive validity in the seemingly random, infinitely complex, world of classroom life. Our point is not at all to disparage educational or psychological research. On the contrary, we find it quite helpful when it is done well. It is the misapplication of research findings that bothers us. It is the misapplication of research findings that should bother you. What we wish to say is that the claims made by someone who says "The research shows . . ." must be carefully considered before we enter into wholesale policy or curriculum change.

The business of teaching and learning in school settings is a very serious trust. All of the involved in the work of schools must do our best to honor that trust. We know that all is not well in the world of learning in America. As educators we are very vulnerable to new nostrums and fixes that will make things right at last. Change is a necessary condition of progress, and it behooves us to make the most meaningful changes possible. Our hope is that as you examine the various attempts at innovation found in this book, you will learn to ask the right questions and that you will find useful answers.

REFERENCES

Slavin, R. (1989), "PET and the Pendulum: Fadism in Education and How to Stop It," *Phi Delta Kappan, 70,* 752-758.

CHAPTER THREE

"THE RESEARCH SAYS . . ."

"There aren't any embarrassing questions—just embarrassing answers."

Carl Rowan

Have you ever found yourself at a meeting or conference listening to a speaker who pauses dramatically and states, in august tones, "Well, the research says . . .?" Everyone, including perhaps yourself, quickly puts pen to paper in anticipation of some significant bombshell that will change school life for ever more. If only you or we had a nickel for every time an education hustler has used such a phrase! If only it were as significant a statement as it appears to be to the uninitiated. The only appropriate response that comes to mind in the midst of such confusion is "What research?"

In fact the claim of virtually all innovators or purveyors of innovation is that research has in some strategic way played an important part in the evolution and development of their ideas, programs, or materials. And, in some sense, the claim is generally true, but often misleading. For example, if someone claims his/her program for elementary children is based in part on learning transfer, we may be impressed. After all, the concept of transfer of learning is well documented in the annals of psychological research. But the jump from research in a laboratory setting to classroom application is a long jump.

WHAT "KIND" OF RESEARCH?

We propose to show you a classification system that should prove helpful as you attempt to sort out the different kinds of research that is conducted. With this knowledge you should be able to determine for yourself what is behind the statement "The research says . . . ."

In essence, there are three levels of research that have implications for educational innovation. The first is basic or pure research done in laboratory settings, the second is applied research done in school settings, and the third is evaluation research applied to school programs. Each is quite different from the others, and each yields its own unique types of conclusions (*see* Figure 3.1).

Level 1 Research

Level 1 research is basic or pure research on learning and behavior. It is most commonly conducted in laboratory settings by psychologists, learning theorists, linguists, etc. Its purpose is to establish a theoretical construct or idea as having some validity. For example, Jean Piaget constructed a theory of stages of intellectual development through which children pass on their way to adult thought (Piaget (1960)). Jerome Bruner constructed a theory of the structure of knowledge which included alternative ways by which knowledge of some reality could be represented to learners (Bruner (1966)). And Howard Gardner has constructed a theory of multiple intelligences (Gardner (1986)).

Although level 1 research can serve as a foundation for curriculum development, it is not designed to answer applied educational questions. Now when Piaget claimed on the basis of his research that most eight year olds are in a stage of concrete operations, many builders of experimental curriculum packages decided to put together mathematics and science activities that involved manipulative materials. And, rightly or wrongly, they did that on the assumption that the message from pure research could be applied to groups of 25 or 30

Figure 3.1. The Three Levels of Educational Research

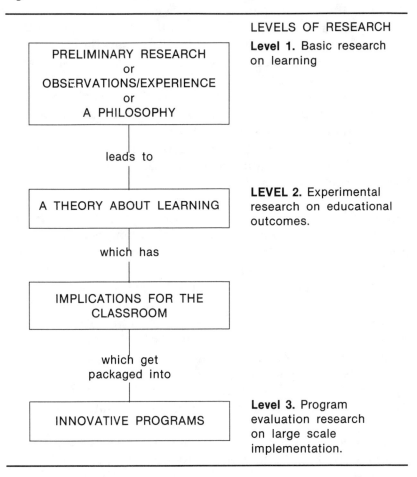

children learning together in a classroom setting. The extent to which it is reasonable to do this is really a function of level 2 research.

Level 2 Research

Level 2 research involves studies the purpose of which is to determine the efficacy of particular programs or instructional methods, etc., in educational settings. Such studies are generally conducted by educational researchers who are interested in applying theories and procedures developed at the pure or basic level. For example, an educational researcher might attempt to set up controlled conditions in several classrooms for the purpose of comparing, say, cooperative learning in social studies with independent student learning. The experimental conditions might call for randomly assigning students and teachers to different treatment modes or conditions where the same material is studied. Pre and post tests may be administered to all participants and comparisons made to determine whether a statistically significant difference occurred between and among treatments.

Level 2 research is applied research because (1) it is conducted in the same or similar settings that are actually found in schools, and (2) it makes no attempt to develop a theory but rather attempts to make instructional or curricular applications of a given theory. At its best, level 2 research provides practical insights that cannot be derived directly from pure research. Thus, even though we all can agree that reinforcement has been shown to be a powerful psychological concept by pure researchers, it remains for the level 2 researcher to demonstrate how it might be advantageous to apply reinforcement in teaching in classroom settings.

Level 2 research is crucial to the process of validation of programs or methods of instruction. But time and time again, this step is simply ignored or poorly crafted as program developers or purveyors tout their product. To return to the ITIP or PET "theory into practice" model for a moment, we can see in retrospect that it claimed its validity on the basis of such pure or basic research constructs as reinforcement, transfer, retention, etc., which are real enough. But it was almost totally lacking in any proof of what happens when you take those constructs and package them up for use by teachers in classroom settings. The same thing can be said for a number of other programs that have swept the country, *e.g.*, "Assertive Discipline," "TESA," and higher level thinking strategies.

One of the best sources for school personnel to search at level 2 is the journal *Review of Educational Research*. This journal carries reviews and meta analyses of various programs, projects, and packages. If nothing else, it will give you insight into the sheer amount of applied research that has or has not been conducted in a given area.

A final point about level 2 research is that each study, even if it represents good research, is severely limited in its generalizability. If, for example, a study of teaching methods of reading and literature were conducted with fourth grade inner city children, then whatever the results, it would be unwise to generalize them to rural eighth grade students. And this is why large numbers of good investigations about a given program should be carried out before school districts jump on this or that bandwagon. Cooperative learning, in our opinion, has been investigated in such a wide variety of school-based settings that its level 2 foundation is quite secure, especially compared to most other innovations.

Level 3 Research

Level 3 research is evaluation research designed to determine the efficacy of programs at the level of school or district implementation. It is by far the least likely of the three types to be carried out in any systematic way, and because of this programs (good, bad, or indifferent) usually just go away in time, replaced by the latest fad.

Examples of level 3 research include evaluation studies that examine the overall effects on teachers and students of a particular district- or school-wide innovation. If a district changes over from basal reading instruction to whole language learning, for example, it is the job of evaluation researchers to determine exactly what changes were brought about and what the results of those changes were. This might involve interviews with teachers, students, and parents, the application of classroom environmental scales to determine student perceptions of whole language learning, examinations of achievement data, and observations in classrooms to document exactly how the new program is being implemented.

A generation ago, when the New Math swept the country, it had a pretty firm foundation at levels 1 and 2, but what little evidence we did gain at level 3 showed us that teachers were actually subverting the New Math, preferring to bring in the Old Math in its place whenever they could.

So, even if you are convinced that the theory behind some new program is sound, and even if you have seen reported evidence of controlled studies in classroom settings that are supportive of the theory's application, you're still not home free until you have seen the results of evaluation studies that indicate that this program really works in large numbers of regular classrooms.

Now you may be thinking that this represents quite a few gates for a new program to have to open before it proves its worth. And that is exactly the point! If we are to become less susceptible to fads, then it will be because we became more deliberate and cautious along the way to adopting new programs.

Figure 3.1 illustrates the process which ideally unfolds in the cycle of educational innovation. We begin with theories derived from pure or basic research. We then test the theory under experimental or quasi-experimental conditions in school settings. And we move from there to the program evaluation stage where assessment is made based on data from real classrooms which operate under typical day-to-day conditions.

SUMMARY

In the world of prescription medications, the Food and Drug Administration (FDA) subjects new medicines to a long and exhaustive review prior to allowing them to be prescribed by doctors and dispensed by pharmacists. Some critics of this system have pointed out that in many cases it takes years from the time we read about an experimental drug in the newspapers and that drug's release to the market. The role of the FDA is to play gatekeeper as tests are conducted, effects examined, potential drug interactions investigated, and so on. As a result, some drugs never make it to the marketplace and some do after a period of time.

With respect to educational innovations, however, we have no counterpart to the FDA. Therefore, programs can be rushed into the schools with little or no testing at any stage of the game. This may please those who are in a hurry to jump on the latest bandwagon, but it disadvantages those who would prefer to be consumers of thoughtfully tested and refined programs. In so many instances, whole districts have adopted particular curriculums and teaching procedures that had basically no research foundation. This renders our profession vulnerable to criticisms that are difficult to refute.

In this chapter we suggested that research ought to be conducted at three distinctly different levels along the way to validating or invalidating educational innovations. Those three levels are comprised of (1) basic or pure research, (2) applied research in school settings, and (3) evaluation research where the effects of the large scale implementation of an innovation are studied. All of this takes time, and rightly so. We think that the only way to improve educational practice is to approach educational innovation with such a deliberate, measured sense of its worth.

Of course, schools adopt new ideas on the basis of something more than educational research. Economic, political, and cultural considerations will always play a role in this process. We have no problem with that. That is part of your reality and ours. But where we can be more thoughtful about change on the basis of a thorough examination of the merits of a given change, we ought to proceed cautiously.

Years ago there was a show on the radio called "It Pays to Be Ignorant." The theory behind the show was that people could win cash prizes and major household appliances by proving to the world, or at least to the huge nationwide radio audience, they really were ignorant when it came to answering questions put to them by the genial host of the show. It was a great concept and a successful program. But we wish to say as clearly as possible that it doesn't pay to be ignorant when it comes to spending the public's tax dollars on educational innovations that really haven't proven themselves!

THE FOLLOWING CHAPTERS

In this book we have attempted to provide teachers, administrators, district inservice personnel, graduate students, and other interested persons with a brief overview of current innovations in education. In the process of selecting these topics we looked carefully at a wide variety of state and school district inservice offerings, college and university courses, and staff development institutes. During this process it became obvious to us that many of the offerings were simply variations of a more limited number of basic ideas or concepts. It is these basic concepts, or golden threads, on which we have tried to focus the following chapters. Of course we recognize that the manifestation of the concepts may differ somewhat from one region of the country to another, or from one packager to another. We will, however, focus only on programs that have truly nationwide impact, whatever their regional calling cards happen to be.

For each of the following chapters we have constructed a common format for our presentation of the topic under review. We begin each chapter with an overview of the concept in an attempt to clarify exactly what is being talked about. We have depended heavily on primary sources for these sections. At times, this has required synthesizing the writing and ideas of numerous authors because for many of these topics there is no single developer who speaks for or represents the entire area. For example, the learning styles movement in education is not dependent on the work of one person; rather it represents a compilation of ideas from numerous investigators and promoters. Even in the instances where one individual is clearly identified with the topic, *e.g.*, Madeline Hunter for the "Hunter Model," we have expanded our discussions past that individual to include descriptions of the programs as they are being implemented and expanded by others. We have attempted to identify the "main players" in each particular field of endeavor, that is, those most closely associated with the topic and related programs. While we may refer to various individuals and their programs as examples, the interpretations and descriptions of the concepts and programs are ours alone.

We have also provided specific examples of the structural effects these programs have, or would have if implemented, in the schools. For example, a teacher who adopts a whole language approach for the classroom, will organize (1) the classroom, (2) the curriculum, and (3) instruction differently from a teacher following, say, a basal-reader approach. Similarly, a school following an outcome-based education model will have a different focus and decision-making process from that found in a goal-free approach to schooling. In each of these chapters we have attempted to show in specific terms what changes will occur if you implement a given program. In other words, ideas have consequences when they become reality, and we wish to be clear about that with you.

Included in each chapter is a critique of the given topic. It is fair to say that the work of the proponents of these ideas and programs is not above criticism, and we are not at all reluctant to do just that. Some programs have been carefully developed and come complete with a sound research foundation. Others are "faddish" and are lacking both a theoretical and research base. In some cases, certain programs are antithetical to each other and the attempt to adopt both or to blend them will lead only to a confusion of purpose. We will be clear about the cautionary notes that are necessary before wholesale changes in an educational system are undertaken. Who knows but what you are presently doing may in fact be better than what will happen if you implement a certain highly touted program.

We also examine proponents' claims about the degree to which the programs are "research-based." The term "research-based" is a little like the term "cholesterol free" found on product labels. It can be rather misleading. At the very least, one must know how to interpret it. And we conclude each chapter with a brief bibliography for those who wish to pursue the issues further.

REFERENCES

Bruner, J. (1966), *Toward a Theory of Instruction*, Cambridge, Massachusetts: Harvard University Press.

Gardner, H. (1986), *Frames of Mind*, New York: Basic Books.

Piaget, J. (1960), *The Child's Conceptions of the World*, Atlantic Highlands, N.J.: Humanities Press, Inc.

CHAPTER FOUR

WHOLE LANGUAGE
LEARNING

"Whole Language — two words that have become a label for an exciting grass–roots teacher movement that is changing curricula around the world. . . . Never in the history of literacy education has there been such genuine excitement on the part of educators."

Dorothy Watson

"It is clear to an observer of the state of reading education in 1990 that the whole language movement is 'riding the pendulum,' in Slavin's (1989) description of the course of educational fads."

Steven Stahl

W hole language is a philosophy of how literacy best develops in learners. It represents a perspective on language and learning which is founded primarily on the use of literature programs, big books, predictable books, book discussion groups, authentic stories rather than basal readers, acceptance of developmental spelling, emphasis on the writing process, etc. It is based on the premise that human beings "acquire language through actually using it for a purpose, not through practicing its separate parts until some later date when the parts are assembled and the totality is finally used" (Altwerger, Edelsky, and Flores (1987), p. 145).

Whole language has emerged as a force in the school curriculum for at least two reasons. One reason is a reaction to the skills-based language programs with their heavy emphasis on the technical (phonics, grammar, correct spelling, etc.) rather than the conceptual aspects of learning. The other reason is that new theories of learning have emerged in recent years, and whole language advocates have been encouraged by those these developments.

Whole language is rooted in part in a learning theory called constructivism. Constructivism is based on the premise that all knowledge is constructed by the learner, and therefore, learning is an intensely personal affair. No two people can or should construct the same knowledge (although it might be quite similar) because each of us has our own unique experiences, our own schema or knowledge structure, our own learning styles, and our own particular motivation to learn.

Because this is so, the thinking goes, it is more appropriate to expose learners to broad ideas than to particular skills. The former permits individual accommodation while the latter assumes that everyone (at least within a group) needs the same thing. And that same thing is a reductionist approach to learning as opposed to a wholistic approach to learning. Of course, this is somewhat of an oversimplification since whole language advocates have rarely said that the teaching of basic reading and grammar skills is always inappropriate. What we talking about here are points of emphasis.

Some observers have noted the similarities between whole language and an approach that was popular a generation ago called language experience. Language experience was based on the premise that reading and writing should come primarily from the child's own experience. For example, a teacher takes the class for a walk around the environs of the school, and afterwards, using large pages of newsprint and felt pen, writes a story that the children tell based on the experience. The children would then practice reading and illustrating their own story. Often, children in language experience classes would write and illustrate their own "books" which they would share with others or give to their parents, etc. The premise was twofold: That reading and writing go together like hand and glove and that personal experience is the key to becoming a reader or a writer. The idea of "ownership" as a motivating force has been claimed by more than one group over the years. The idea can be traced back at least to Francis Bacon, who said the key to learning was found in experience, one's own and not someone else's.

GRABBING HOLD OF A "SLIPPERY QUARRY"

One of the major problems with the whole language movement is its variety of definitions. It has been described as a "slippery quarry" and as "something hard to measure" (McKenna, Robinson, and Miller (1990)). Even whole language advocates openly admit that the concept is difficult to define and that it defies "a dictionary-type definition." Basically, whole language is a philosophy of teaching and learning that proposes that all language concepts are closely interconnected, that to separate them is artificial, and that they are best learned in a natural or "whole" manner. This description contrasts with the traditional reductionist, skill-focused approach to language where children begin with letters, sounds, blends, phonemes, etc., or what one proponent of whole language calls "barking at text." Instead whole language flows from the child's personal, natural language patterns and with the reading and writing of stories and other forms of literature which draw upon the child's experience.

Several terms are closely associated with whole language learning. One of those terms is "meaning centered." A meaning centered approach seeks relevance and avoids isolated skills as the road to literacy. Another term found in the repertoire of whole language advocates is "integration." Since language is the root of much of our learning, whole language classrooms provide language experiences as a fundamental part of all the curriculums. And a third term is "natural learning." We don't directly teach people to walk or even to talk. It happens along the way in a supportive environment. By analogy, the argument goes, so should learning to read and write be made as natural as possible. Figure 4.1 illustrates the set of common assumptions and beliefs held by whole language advocates.

An integral component of whole language philosophy is the nurturing of the natural process by which a child comes to think about language as a result of his/her prior knowledge and life experiences. Perhaps in the most fundamental sense of learning, the difference between whole language and tradi-

Figure 4.1.   Common Beliefs of Whole Language Advocates

STUDENTS CONSTRUCT THEIR OWN KNOWLEDGE FROM WITHIN.
They use their prior knowledge to construct new knowledge.
Knowledge is not something poured directly into their heads by
some external source. Teachers, therefore, continuously provide
opportunities for students to use knowledge they already have
and to take an active role in their own learning.

**LITERACY ACTIVITY SHOULD BE A NATURAL OUTGROWTH OF THE
INTERESTS OF STUDENTS.** Instead of engaging in predetermined
language arts activities, students select a significant amount of
their own reading materials and write about topics of interest to
them.

**READING IS COMPREHENSION – THAT IS, CREATING MEANING
FROM TEXT. IT IS NOT A SET OF HIERARCHICALLY ARRANGED
SUBSKILLS TO BE MASTERED.** The focus of teaching reading is
on readers creating meaning as they read. Growth in reading
takes place as students read and write whole and meaningful
texts.

COMMUNICATION IS THE MAIN GOAL OF WRITING. Becoming a
good writer requires engagement in the process of writing and
the support of teachers and peers. Whole-language teachers let
students select their own writing topics, accept their attempts to
express themselves, and make certain they have an audience for
sharing their writing.

LEARNING TO READ AND WRITE IS A SOCIAL PROCESS. An
exchange of points of view contributes significantly to students'
construction of knowledge; they think critically when they defend
their own ideas and listen to other points of view. Whole-language
teachers arrange for students to interact with one another about
their reading and writing.

**RISK TAKING AND MAKING MISTAKES ARE CRITICAL TO GROWTH
IN READING AND WRITING.** Making errors is a natural part of
learning as students go through various levels of being "wrong."
In this way, they construct their coherent systems of written language. Whole-language teachers encourage students to be autonomous, self-directed learners who view mistakes as a necessary
part of learning.

Source: Manning, Gary; Manning, Maryann; and Long, Roberta, *Reading and Writing
in the Middle Grades: A Whole-Language View,* Washington, DC: National Education
Association (1990), pp. 8-9.

tional language programs is that whole language emphasizes whole-to-part learning while traditional forms emphasize part-to-whole learning. In other words, they are diametrically opposing points of view.

WHOLE LANGUAGE IN THE CLASSROOM

In whole language, phonics and word drills are downplayed. Instead the student is encouraged to learn to read and write much as he/she learned to speak, naturally. Emphasis is placed on encouragement with a focus on success in a natural setting rather than on errors, corrections of mistakes, and "word attack" skills. It is believed by whole language advocates that not only will the child more readily learn in a rich literary environment that encourages and "celebrates" reading and writing, but that he/she will *want* to read and write as a result. Intrinsic motivation and relevance are stressed as the teacher facilitates, rather than directs the learning process.

Teachers who consider themselves to be users of the whole language approach fall into several categories. Purists tend to eschew basic skills approaches altogether, while eclecticists try to accommodate a blend of whole language and traditional reading and writing instruction. A more all-encompassing position tends to take whole language to the limits, making it an entire curriculum as the classroom takes on the trappings of open education. But most users of whole language focus its use on the more conventional areas of the language arts curriculum.

School districts that choose whole language programs often require experienced teachers to take some training designed to move them from the traditional approach to language arts to the whole language approach. Prospective teachers in such districts are often screened on the basis of their knowledge of and willingness to use whole language. The chart in Figure 4.2 illustrates some of the differences between traditional and whole language views of the curriculum. A review of the elements of curriculum and instruction found in Figure 4.2 reveal that a fundamental difference is found between the two

Figure 4.2. Classroom Implications for Contrasting Views of Education

	Traditional	*Whole Language*
Learning Goals	Specific objectives in each subject area, usually identified by the school, district, or state. The objectives are hierarchical and tied to textbooks or teacher guides. The focus is on the product, with particular emphasis given to a student's deficits.	Teachers work with students to create a curriculum based on the interests and strengths of the individual student. Learning focuses on the process and learning in a functional context.
Teacher Role	A transmitter of information with major responsibility for determining what and how students should learn.	A facilitator of learning helping the student with the process of learning, sharing responsibility for learning with the student.
Materials	Basal readers, skill books and worksheets, social studies, math, language, science textbooks.	Student-selected reading materials, meaningful projects involving a variety of integrated materials from the various disciplines.
Class Structure and Activities	Students in traditional rows, with direct instruction predominant. Students may be grouped by achievement level. Minimal use of group learning activities. Teaching of skills in isolation from other parts of the curriculum with separate periods of the day for the various subjects.	Variable seating arrangements with considerable flexibility. Subjects integrated with language and reading, with considerable group and cooperative learning activities. Limited direct instruction or only when the need arises within the context of the learning activities at a meaningful time.
Evaluation	Standardized tests, workbooks, worksheets; teacher-made tests which evaluate isolated skills mastery. The frame of reference for evaluation is an external standard or group norm.	Teacher observations of the learning process, writing samples, student self-evaluation, portfolios. The student is evaluated against his/herself to identify growth in various areas.

approaches with respect to learning goals, teacher role, student activities, materials used, methods of assessment, and the very structure of the classroom. Needless to say, any teacher, principal, or whole district that contemplates such a basic change should be well aware of the implications, and should be able to defend such a change to parents and other interested parties.

THE RESEARCH BASE FOR WHOLE LANGUAGE

Whole language advocates claim that "the research base for whole language philosophy is broad and multidisciplinary. It includes research in linguistics, psycholinguistics, sociology, anthropology, philosophy, child development, curriculum, composition, literary theory, semiotics, and other fields of study." (Newman and Church (1989), p. 20.) Such a broad based claim is overwhelming, and it might lead one to say that the evidence in favor of whole language is incontrovertible.

In the book *The Administrator's Guide to Whole Language* (Heald-Taylor (1989)), an entire chapter is devoted to whole language research. Allusions are made to some 50 studies which cover a range of related topics including writing, oral language, reading, and developmental studies. This apparently is the research base for whole language learning. Prominent among the researchers cited are Kenneth Goodman, Donald Graves, Delores Durkin, Marie Clay, and Frank Smith.

Our conclusion is that whole language has indeed a credible pure or basic (level 1) research foundation. Furthermore, the philosophical basis of whole language is one of a clearly thought out theory of learning. Thus, the basic research and the theoretical model are sound. They have been used to give direction to teaching/learning practices at the classroom level. It is at this level, that of implementation, that the grounds for whole language appear somewhat shaky.

The practical questions are: "Do students learn more in whole language classrooms?" and "Is the learning qualitatively improved in whole language classrooms?" This is the domain of applied research (level 2). Our answer to those questions is that evidence is lacking. Let us see why this is so.

HOW DO WE DO IT?

Empirical researchers have observed that investigating the effect of whole language instruction is difficult because of the lack of an agreed upon definition of whole language. As we suggested previously, people mean different things when they use the term. It should also be noted that a number of whole language advocates claim that "traditional" methods of assessment are inappropriate when it comes to evaluating this approach to teaching and learning. (McKenna, Robinson, Miller (1990a), p. 4.)

McKenna, Robinson, and Miller have suggested a cooperative research agenda designed to treat these problems. They propose that the following eight steps be taken:

- The concept must be defined to enable researchers to know whether a program represents whole language or not, or at least how to categorize a given program;

- Both experimental and quasi-experimental research is needed;

- Qualitative studies should also be employed;

- The effects on student attitudes should be studied;

- Longitudinal studies should be undertaken;

- Learner characteristics as they interact with traditional and whole language instruction should be identified;

- Studies should identify the role of teacher variables in instruction;

- Collaborative research partnerships between researchers and whole language advocates should be developed.

Of course, this agenda is needed not merely for whole language program assessment but for program assessment in general.

Some whole language advocates, however, take strong exception to the idea of such a research agenda. In an article titled

"Whose Agenda Is This, Anyway?," Carole Edelsky (1990) wrote that traditional research forms have little relevance to whole language because "two competing views are more than different 'takes' on language arts instruction; they are conflicting educational paradigms. Each uses different discourse; maintains different values; and emanates from a different educational community" (p. 7). In a response to her response, McKenna *et al.* wrote: "[I]n essence, people share a system of beliefs and they claim they have evidence to support their beliefs. But, when you look up what they [whole language advocates] cite as evidence, it is often just someone else's published beliefs." (McKenna, Robinson, and Miller (1990b), p. 12.)

In fairness, it should be stated that whole language advocates are not necessarily opposed to any form of evaluation research. Rather they question the appropriateness of the measures used which are, typically, standardized tests. Such tests, whole language proponents claim, isolate learning in bits and pieces and ask children to show their knowledge in unnatural settings.

What kinds of program evaluation do whole language proponents advocate? First of all, they would propose that qualitative research, rather than quantitative, be emphasized. They suggest that writing samples which could be judged as process rather than product would be a place to start. Also, they are very interested in determining students' attitudes toward learning to read and write. In order to get a sense of students' attitudes, it would be necessary to conduct personal interviews and to employ other, similar qualitative data gathering procedures. Basically, whole language advocates feel that placing the assessment marbles in the quantitative/product bag is a mistake which leads to irrelevant conclusions about student learning. This leaves the potential consumer in a quandary because we can all appreciate the sensitivity toward attitude development and the employment of more "natural" measures of achievement. On the other hand, it is much easier to compare quantitative achievement results between this reading program and that when districts are faced with the expensive decisions associated with program adoption and implementation.

WHAT WE DO KNOW

In spite of all this, what does the research we *do* have say about the effectiveness of whole language programs? The most comprehensive review of the research on whole language effectiveness was conducted by Steven A. Stahl and Patricia D. Miller (1989). Their review included both quantitative and naturalistic or qualitative studies. Stahl and Miller write: "Our review . . . concludes that we have no evidence showing that whole language programs produce effects that are stronger than existing basal programs, and potentially may produce lower effects. The alternative, that whole language programs are too new to evaluate, also suggests a lack of evidence of their efficacy. In short, both views foster doubt as to the prudence of a widespread adoption of such an approach, pending evidence of its effectiveness." (Stahl (1990), p. 143.)

This review of whole language research outcomes is not without its critics. Members of the whole language community rejected its definitions of whole language and the methodologies of the research itself (Schickendanz (1990); McGee and Lomax (1990)). So where does this leave us?

Interestingly, none of the research in the meta-analysis by Stahl and Miller was in the research chapter of *The Administrator's Guide to Whole Language* (Heald-Taylor (1989)). The *Guide* contained only two comparative studies, both small-scale and informal, which showed that whole language increased learning.

A few studies have appeared since the meta-analysis by Stahl and Miller, and they tend to show mixed, inconclusive results. One of those studies, however, shows some promise for whole language, or at least whole language defined in a limited sense as the combination of literature-based and basal-reader instruction. A thoughtful, well-designed study conducted by Lesley Mandel Morrow concluded that

> the combination of literature-based instruction with traditional basal reading instruction is more powerful than traditional instruction alone. (Morrow (1992), p. 273.)

Morrow went on to say that "although there is a great deal of anecdotal data concerning the benefits of using literature in reading instruction, *only a few empirical studies exist*" [emphasis added] (Morrow (1992), p. 273).

So whole language advocates continue to tout their approach on the basis of enthusiasm and testimonials. While enthusiasm and testimonials are significant and should not be cynically cast aside, they may not be enough to go on when it comes to spending big money on new programs and teacher retraining. We simply are lacking the evidence necessary to state that schools that wish to improve test scores in the areas of the language arts should adopt the whole language approach. But here's the rub: Raising standardized test scores conflicts with goals and objectives held by whole language advocates. So those who choose to adopt a whole language approach to language arts must do so for reasons they find compelling, and those reasons will have to be sought in sources beyond the empirical record as it exists to date.

Certainly, in the annals of Progressive Education one finds compelling reasons for integrating the course of study, getting children involved in experiential learning, and reading "real" books rather than basal readers. These are hallmarks of whole language learning that we find rather appealing. In that sense the whole language approach seems commendable. So much of the joy of childhood is taken away when we focus on task-oriented, teacher-imposed "basic skills" learning. Whole language is dedicated to celebrating each child's quest for personal growth, and that is not a bad goal.

REFERENCES

Altwerger, B., Edelsky, C., and Flores, B. (1987), "Whole Language: What's New?," *The Reading Teacher*, 41(2), 144-154.

Cambourne, B. (1988), *The Whole Story*, Auckland, New Zealand: Ashton Scholastic.

Edelsky, C. (1990), "Whose Agenda is this Anyway? A Response to McKenna, Robinson, and Miller," *Educational Researcher*, 19(8), 7-11.

Edelsky, C., Altwerger, B., and Flores, B. (1991), *Whole Language: What's the Difference?*, Portsmouth, NH: Heinemann.

Heald-Taylor, G. (1989), *The Administrator's Guide to Whole Language*, Rich C. Owen Publisher.

Goodman, K.S. (1989), "Whole-language Research: Foundations and Development," *The Elementary School Journal*, 90(2), 207-221.

Goodman, Y.M. (1989), "Roots of the Whole Language Movement," *The Elementary School Journal*, 90(2), 113-127.

Manning, G., Manning, M., and Long, R. (1990), *Reading and Writing in the Middle Grades: A Whole-Language View*, Washington, DC: National Education Association.

McGee, L.M., and Lomax, R.S. (1990), "On Combining Apples and Oranges: A Response to Stahl and Miller," *Review of Educational Research*, 60(1), 133-140.

McKenna, M.C., Robinson, R.D., and Miller, J.W. (1990a), "Whole Language: A Research Agenda for the Nineties," *Educational Researcher*, 19(8), 3-6.

McKenna, M.C., Robinson, R.D., and Miller, J.W. (1990b), "Whole Language and the Need for Open Inquiry: A Rejoinder to Edelsky," *Educational Researcher*, 19(8), 12-13.

Morrow, L.M. (1992), "The Impact of a Literature-based Program on Literacy Achievement, Use of Literature and Attitudes of Children from Minority Backgrounds," *Reading Research Quarterly*, 27(3), p. 251-275.

Newman, J.M., and Church, S.M. (1989), "Myths of Whole Language," *The Reading Teacher*, 44(1), 20-26.

Schickendanz, J.A. (1990), "The Jury is Still Out on the Effects of Whole Language and Language Experience Approaches for Beginning Reading: A Critique of Stahl and Miller's Study," *Review of Educational Research*, 60(1), 127-131.

Stahl, S. (1990), "Riding the Pendulum: A Rejoinder to Schickedanz and McGee and Lomax," *Review of Educational Research*, 60(1), 141-151.

Stahl, S.A., and Miller, P.D. (1989), "Whole Language and Language Experience Approaches for Beginning Reading: A Quantitative Research Synthesis," *Review of Educational Research*, 59(1), 87-116.

Watson, D. (1990), "Defining and Describing Whole Language," *The Elementary School Journal*, 90(2), p. 129-141.

CHAPTER FIVE

INNOVATIONS FROM BRAIN RESEARCH

"Recent dramatic advances in the neurosciences and in cognitive psychology are moving us toward a clearer understanding of the three-pound human brain that is the focus of our profession."

Robert Sylwester

"I think a lot of the research is suspect. We have much to learn before we run amok with homemade conclusions and consequent activities built on our interpretation of brain research data."

Anthony Gregorc

The current love affair on the part of Education with brain research flows from the belief that if we can figure out how the brain functions, that is, how information is received, stored, retrieved and otherwise processed, we can then design educational programs based on that knowledge. Brain research represents for many the ultimate pedagogical frontier. Once this new territory is explored and mapped, the promise of maximizing the learning potential of each student will be realized.

The basic research in this area began with Paul Broca's celebrated 19th Century theory of hemispheric dominance. Research into brain function has continued apace in the 20th Century. In 1981 Roger Sperry received the Nobel Prize for his split-brain research. Most educational claims are based on this and other medical research. As we shall see, researchers have done little to support the teaching/learning generalizations put forth by advocates and promoters (Reiff (1992), Carnine (1990), Curry (1990); Springer and Deutsch (1989); Wittrock (1981)).

There are a variety of theories and ideas that have emerged from the basic research into brain function. However, they seem to coalesce around two major concepts: Hemisphericity and growth spurts.

Sperry's research supports the idea that the two hemispheres of the brain serve differing but complementary functions. A person uses both hemispheres when learning or functioning, but one may dominate the other and determine a person's style or preferred way of learning. Each hemisphere is thought to contribute specialized functions to tasks. The left hemisphere of the brain is associated with verbal, sequential, analytical abilities. The right hemisphere is associated with global, holistic, visual-spatial abilities. Two related ideas are full *lateralization*, when the left hemisphere dominates in language expression while the right hemisphere dominates in nonverbal processing, and *parallel processing*, a research finding that indicates that the brain hemispheres perform many tasks simultaneously.

Herman Epstein's medical research, done in the 1970's, seems to indicate that the brain grows in spurts rather than in a continual, uninterrupted process. This finding is often used to support the Piagetian model of cognitive development. Growth spurts in school age children often occur between the ages of 6-8, 10-12, and 14-16. And they often occur in summer when school is not in session. Myelination has to do with the process of nerve fiber maturation which occurs in stages that seem to parallel Piagetian stages of cognitive growth and development. Connecting nerve systems are the last to myelineate in childhood, indicating that a child could be said to have a "functionally split brain."

There are a number of other areas of brain research that may well have educational implications, but they remain beyond our pedagogical grasp simply because the medical knowledge itself is still quite limited. These include endorphin molecules, memory, hyperactivity, attention span, creativity, and others. Just to cite an example, researchers at the UCLA Medical Center have discovered that children below the age of 10 have brain activity that is unusually rich in the secretion of theta waves, thought to be associated with creativity. Whether this knowledge will in the future stop teachers from handing out worksheet after worksheet to these naturally creative little characters remains the object of future speculation. The general opinion of experts is that at this time we have barely scratched the surface in our knowledge of the human brain.

THE PENDULUM HAS STARTED ITS SWING

From the various medical findings a wide range of educational theories has emerged. Robert Sylwester wrote that "The brain is the most magnificent three pounds of matter in the universe. What we now know about the human brain and what we'll discover in the years ahead may well transform formal education" (Sylwester (1981)). Whether what we think we know about the brain will prove useful or not, educators have jumped on the bandwagon with article after article about the educational implications of medical research. Sylwester, one of the leading educational authorities on the teaching/learning implications of brain research, wrote as far back as 1981:

> ". . . but can we afford to wait until all problems are solved before we begin to study the education issues implicit in this research? When mass media begin to report discoveries, parents will expect us to respond" (Sylwester (1981), p. 8).

In at least a comparative sense, Sylwester was cautious, believing that it was too early to implement curricular and instructional changes based on the medical research. Other educators were less reserved. It is fair to say that many educators have responded to the medical findings by developing theories and strategies designed to influence life in classrooms. The topic has become a common offering for staff development workshops.

An example of learning implications derived from medical research is reflected in the work of Caine and Caine (1990). They write that they have developed "brain principles as a general theoretical foundation for brain-based learning. These principles are simple and neurologically sound. Applied to education, however, they help us to reconceptualize teaching by taking us out of traditional frames of reference and guiding us in defining and selecting appropriate programs and methodologies" ((1990), p. 66).

A summary of Caine and Caine's brain-based learning theory is presented in Figure 5.1. Each of the 12 learning principles has direct implications for teaching and learning. For example, Principle Two states that "brain-based teaching must fully incorporate stress management, nutrition, exercise, drug education, and other facets of health into the learning process" (p. 66). Principle Six states that "vocabulary and grammar are best understood and mastered when they are incorporated in genuine, whole-language experiences. Similarly, equations and scientific principles are best dealt with in the context of living science" (p. 67). These are interesting conclusions in any educational context, but to state that they are based on brain research gives them, one supposes, heightened credibility. At any rate, these assertions sailed past the editorial gate keepers of *Educational Leadership*, a policy journal in the field of education.

Figure 5.1.   Caine and Caine's Brain Research Based Learning Principles

---

Principle One: The Brain Is a Parallel Processor.
Principle Two: Learning Engages the Entire Physiology.
Principle Three: The Search for Meaning is Innate.
Principle Four: The Search for Meaning Occurs Through "Patterning."
Principle Five: Emotions Are Critical to Patterning.
Principle Six: Every Brain Simultaneously Perceives and Creates Parts and Wholes.
Principle Seven: Learning Involves Both Focused Attention and Peripheral Perception.
Principle Eight: Learning Always Involves Conscious and Unconscious Processes.
Principle Nine: We Have Two Types of Memory: A Spatial Memory System and a Set of Systems for Rote Learning.
Principle Ten: The Brain Understands and Remembers Best When Facts and Skills Are Embedded in Natural Spatial Memory.
Principle Eleven: Learning Is Enhanced by Challenge and Inhibited by Threat.
Principle Twelve: Each Brain Is Unique.

Source: Caine, R.N., and Caine, G. (1990), "Understanding a Brain-Based Approach to Learning and Teaching," *Educational Leadership*, 48(2), 66–70.

The application of basic brain research to education has also resulted in an emphasis on learning styles, particularly among proponents of hemisphericity (right and left brain preference) in learning. We will treat learning styles as a separate topic in the following chapter. However, it is worth noting that both learning styles advocates and brain research educators support a whole-brain approach to teaching. That is, they both claim that it is necessary to teach to both sides of the brain thereby providing a wide and complementary range of strategies and activities to stimulate learners.

Bernice McCarthy's 4MAT System (1987) is an example of a hybrid program that incorporates brain research and learning styles. McCarthy developed a comprehensive instructional approach to meeting individual needs by combining research on brain hemispheres with David Kolb's Learning Cycle (1985). The 4MAT System identifies the learning needs of four types of learners and accompanying strategies for the integration of both right and left brain processing skills.

Other educational implications cited by brain-based teaching advocates include:

* Balanced teaching in order to engage both hemispheres;

* Growth spurts and their implications for individualization, pacing, year-round schooling, acceleration, and failure policies;

* Matching structure and content of curricula, environments, activities, and interactions to cognitive abilities;

* Curriculum integration to provide meaningful contexts and connections among and between subjects;

* Schema theory, to furnish a learning environment that provides stability and familiarity as well as challenge and discovery;

* Wider ranges of contextual and sensory cues in learning in order to increase the number of links made with each new concept, thus leading to improved long term memory and transfer.

RESEARCH ON EDUCATION AND THE BRAIN

The research at level 1 is classic basic research into brain function. The researchers themselves admit that the research base is just developing and that it has barely scratched the surface. The concept of different functions for the two hemispheres of the brain is widely accepted with the left brain controlling linear activity and the right brain controlling global activity. Tests have been devised to document these functions. It has also been documented that brain growth in children occurs in spurts rather than as a continuous activity. Research continues in the areas we mentioned previously: endorphin molecules, theta wave production, memory function, hyperactivity, attention, etc.

The findings resulting from pure research have been examined by certain educators who have linked those findings to a variety of educational implications. It has been postulated, for example (Reiff (1992)), that a teacher's awareness of different modes of learning can help him/her to better teach the whole child. But at research level 2, too few objective, well-designed studies identifying specific educational purposes have been conducted to provide an acceptable and reliable base in support of such claims.

What applied research there is is intertwined with learning styles research and, like learning styles research, is often of poor quality. Level 1 research will continue and, of course, educators will continue to draw inferences for teaching and learning from it. But it is much too early in the movement to point to research that raises test scores, or much of anything else for that matter. Not surprisingly then, we could find no evidence of level 3 program evaluation studies that demonstrate that teacher education or workshop participation in brain research results in better school practice, however one might choose to define it.

CONCLUSIONS

It is probably useful for educators to be informed of the research in brain function. The problem is, however, that it tends to be highly technical research from another field — that of medical research. The extent to which medical research will trickle down to real educational implications remains to be seen. Much of the stuff touted by brain-based teaching advocates resembles good sense teaching, so in that way it may be harmless at worst and useful at best. But we may be a few years away from any major revelations that are directly applicable in classrooms.

Our recommendation is that you attempt to keep informed of developments in this field. The research base at level one will continue to grow exponentially. Our knowledge right now is quite primitive, but it won't stay that way. Look for a host of new insights down the road. The fact that the direct classroom applications are not presently there should not blind us from the realities that will emerge in the future. This area will in time come to have more to offer teaching and learning than we can presently imagine.

REFERENCES

Carnine, D. (1990), "New Research on the Brain: Implications for Instruction," *Phi Delta Kappan*, 71(5), 272-277.

Caine, R.N., and Caine, G. (1990), "Understanding a Brain-Based Approach to Learning and Teaching," *Educational Leadership*, 48(2), 66-70.

Caine, R.N., and Caine, G. (1991), *Making Connections: Teaching and the Human Brain*, Alexandria, VA: Association for Supervison and Curriculum Development.

Garger, S. (1990), "Is There a Link Between Learning Style and Neurophysiology?," *Educational Leadership*, 48(2), 63-65.

Hand, J. (1989), "Split Brain Theory and Recent Results in Brain Research: Implications for the Design of Instruction," in R.K. Bass and C.R. Dills (Eds.), *Instructional Development: The State of the Art, II*, Dubuque, Iowa: Kendall/IIunt.

Kolb, D.A. (1985), *The Learning Style Inventory*, Boston, Mass.: McBer & Co.

Levy, J. (1983), "Research Synthesis on the Right and Left Hemisphere: We Think with Both Sides of the Brain," *Educational Leadership*, 40(2), 4, 66-71.

McCarthy, B. (1987), *The 4MAT System: Teaching to Learning Styles with Right/Left Mode Techniques*, Barrington, Ill.: Excel, Inc.

Reiff, J.C. (1992), *What Research Says to the Teacher: Learning Styles*, Washington DC: National Education Association Professional Library.

Restak, R.M. (1984), *The Brain*, Toronto: Bantam Books.

Springer, S., and Deutsch, G. (1989), *Left Brain Right Brain (3rd ed.)*, New York: W.H. Freeman and Company.

Sylwester, R. (1990), "An Educators Guide to Books on the Brain," *Educational Leadership, 48*(2), 79-80.

CHAPTER SIX

LEARNING STYLES

"Students are not failing because of the curriculum. Students can learn almost any subject matter when they are taught with methods and approaches responsive to their learning style strengths."

Rita Dunn

"Like the blind men in the fable about the elephant, learning styles researchers tend to investigate only a part of the whole and thus have yet to provide a definitive picture of the matter before them."

Lynn Curry

"The idea of learning styles is appealing, but a critical examination of this approach should cause educators to be skeptical."

Vicki E. Snider

The thesis of learning styles is that individuals vary considerably in how they learn. This is to say that any given person has what are called modality strengths that are, one supposes, determined by a combination of hereditary and environmental influences. These modality strengths, which translate into preferences to learn and communicate visually, orally, spatially, tactily, etc., are one's learning style. Beyond that there are some further considerations, for example, whether one learns better in a quiet or busy setting, a formal or relaxed environment, or together or alone.

All of this is quite intriguing, and it has led to the development of a range of models some of which are quite elaborate. Dunn, Dunn, and Price (1979) note that learning style is predicated on "the manner in which at least eighteen different elements from four basic stimuli affect a person's ability to absorb and retain." Other equally complex learning styles models have been developed by Gregoric, McCarthy, and Hunt.

It has been suggested that learning styles are not merely phenomenons of individual differences but that differences are also found among and between cultures. Bennett (1990) has noted that Native American students "approach tasks visually, seem to prefer to learn by careful observation which precedes performance, and seem to learn in their natural settings experientially." Bennett suggests further that African American students tend to be field dependent learners which means that they tend to take their cues from the social environment and that much of their motivation comes from factors external to the material to be learned itself. Added to the cultural dimension is that of social class as a factor in determining how one learns.

Now if this is all true, what we have here is compound interest because the suggestion is that in order to find a given individual in the vast learning matrix, we must determine not merely his/her individual style, but his/her cultural and social context as well. This could lead teachers quickly into a labyrinthine world of diagnosis in the search for style. But it doesn't have to be that complicated, say the purveyors of learning styles.

The National Task Force on Learning Styles and Brain Behavior gives us the following definition of the term learning style:

> "Learning style is that consistent pattern of behavior and performance by which an individual approaches educational experiences. It is the composite of characteristic cognitive, affective, and physiological behaviors that serve as relatively stable indicators of how a learner perceives, interacts with, and responds to the learning environment. It is formed in the deep structure of neural organization and personality [that] molds and is molded by human development and the cultural experiences of home, school, and society" (Bennett, 1990, p. 158).

This definition is quite broad and all-encompassing to say the least. Cornett (1983) offers a similar, simplified definition: "Essentially, learning style can be defined as a consistent pattern of behavior but with a certain range of individual variability. . . ." Guild and Garger (1985) point out that the idea of learning style includes cognitive style, teaching style, leadership style, and psychological type. Figure 6.1 illustrates three areas of style characteristics including cognition, conceptualization, and affect. A review of Figure 6.1 will give you a sense of the characteristics of these broad categories and the researchers who have developed ideas related to them.

It is common to categorize learning styles into some type of taxonomy of human characteristics of learning behavior. The various taxonomies include cognitive, affective, and physiological considerations. Thus, with respect to cognition, a person might exhibit concrete or abstract learning characteristics. With respect to affect, a person might find quite different sources for his/her motivation to learn. And with respect to physiological considerations, a person might have preferences for different light, temperature, and room arrangement.

LEARNING STYLES AND INTELLIGENCE

The essence of learning styles is that each of us receives and processes information differently, and because this is so teachers should make every attempt to know how students learn best. The logic of this thought dictates to us that all styles are equal and that intelligence and ability are equally but differentially distributed among human beings. Typical school assignments tend to discriminate in favor or against certain learners. But the issue may not be one of ability if one person learns much and another little from, say, a particular lecture. It may be, rather, that the lecture format was more suited to one person's learning style than to another's. What this says is that otherwise capable people are left behind in many cases simply because the approach to learning was inappropriate, not because they were incapable of learning the idea.

The relationship between various learning styles and ability to learn subject matter is not well established. It tends to remain, in our opinion, within the realm of speculation. Witkin (1977), a pioneer researcher in this field, maintained that any given style is not superior to another, a proposition that immediately intersects with our ideas of the definition of intelligence. But the problem with this is that the very defini-

Figure 6.1.   Three Areas of Style Characteristics

Category	Characteristics	Researchers
1. *Cognition* — perceiving, finding out, getting information	sensing/ intuition	Jung, Myers-Briggs, Mok, Keirsey and Bates
	field dependent/field independent abstract/ concrete	Witkin, Gregorc, Kolb and McCarthy
	visual, auditory, kinesthetic, tactile	Barbe and Swassing, Dunn and Dunn
2. *Conceptualization* — thinking, forming ideas, processing, memory	extrovert/ introvert	Jung, Myers-Briggs, Keirsey and Bates
	reflective observation/ active experimentation	Kolb and McCarthy
	random/ sequential	Gregorc
3. *Affect* — feelings, emotional response, motivation, values, judgments	feeler/thinker	Jung, Myers-Briggs, Mok, Keirsey and Bates
	effect of temperature, light, food, time of day, sound, design	Dunn and Dunn

Adapted from Guild, P.B., and Garger, S. (1985), *Marching to Different Drummers*, Alexandria, Virginia: Association for Supervision and Curriculum Development, p. 9.

tion of intelligence is being thoughtfully reexamined by such researchers as Howard Gardner (1983), and the chances are that what we presently mean by intelligence as measured by IQ tests and what we will mean by intelligence in the future are two different things. At present analytical ability is considered basic to one's intelligence as measured by IQ tests. Global, intuitive learners tend to score much lower on tests of analytical abilities. Are they therefore less intelligent than analytical thinkers who obviously score higher? Well, it depends on one's definition of intelligence.

IMPLICATIONS FOR THE CLASSROOM

Learning styles advocates point to two major areas of concern for the focus of teachers' energies. Those areas are style assessment and style matching. In other words, what we need to do is discover a learner's style and match how we teach him/her accordingly.

A variety of learning styles assessment instruments exist. They cover all the areas noted in Figure 6.1. Instruments are available for adults as well as for children. The best known instruments include the *Myers-Briggs Type Indicator*, the *Learning Styles Inventory*, and the *Embedded Figures Test*. Because they are tools for assessing one's learning style, the outcome or test result is positive no matter what it is. This seems in some ways a rather curious thing. For example, in the *Embedded Figures Test*, if one is unable to identify certain figures against the background in which they are embedded, it is considered not an inability but rather a global way of looking at things. On the other hand, the ability to identify the various figures merely means one has an analytical approach to learning. This may be one of the first instances in the annals of testing where failure to solve a problem merely puts you in a different but equal category.

In addition to the diagnostic instruments themselves, there are learning styles workbooks that show learners how to identify their styles; and based on the results, the books offer suggestions for how to approach classes and topics, how to study and prepare for exams, and how to deal with teachers whose own teaching styles vary.

The other major issue, matching teachers and students with respect to style, becomes crucial once one has been properly diagnosed. This brings to mind the image created by the old insight that the ideal learning environment would be Mark Hopkins and Teddy Roosevelt sitting on either end of a log conversing with one another. Or one can imagine Aristotle walking through the shaded groves of ancient Athens speaking for the centuries while his eager disciples followed in his wake taking in his every word. Or imagine a little child sitting in mother's lap being told, for the countless time, a certain story. Or imagine the kid who is simply great at arcade games but who has little interest or seemingly little ability to do paper and pencil work.

We could go on, but you get the idea. Each of us probably has some optimum conditions that make learning more meaningful for us.

So the challenge for teachers is to use different modalities, for example, stories, explanations, projects, activities, etc., in order to reach all the different learners in a class effectively, and to use special techniques to meet different styles, for example, overviews for global learners, linear explanations for analytical learners, etc.

Advocates propose a number of teaching strategies that encompass the variety of learning styles. One might say that this is the essence of good teaching anyway. Here is a sample list of ways to reach different styles:

- Using questions at a variety of levels of thinking;

- Providing an overview of material before proceeding to specifics;

- Allowing sufficient time for information to be processed;

- Using examples and activities directed to both left and right hemispheres of the brain;

- Providing set induction and closure activities;

- Setting clear purposes before any listening, viewing, or reading experience;

* Using spaced practice;

* Using multi-sensory means to convey ideas to be learned.

These strategies would probably benefit most learners in most learning situations, and would, according to learning style theory, reach, differentially, all types of learners.

On more narrow grounds, specific strategies are thought to work better with certain styles. *See* Figure 6.2 as an example of instructional strategies designed to meet the needs of field-dependent (global/intuitive) learners. Schools have long been believed to have discriminated against field-dependent learners. Textbooks, workbooks, lectures, explanations, etc., tend, at least traditionally, to be quite linear and analytical in their approaches to knowledge. To overcome this, teachers are urged to use the strategies illustrated in Figure 6.2 because they are particularly appropriate and helpful to global thinkers. Supposedly, we could come up with a list for each style.

THE RESEARCH BASE FOR LEARNING STYLES

The learning styles literature is related to the literature of brain research, but the two movements are not synonymous. The

Figure 6.2. Instructional Strategies for Field-Dependent Learners

---

* Present learning in a global way; focus on the "big picture"; give an overview and the concept.
* Make connections among content, integrate learning, identify relationships among subjects.
* Provide a context for learning and a sense of the purpose of the learning.
* Provide structure, clear expectations, direction and organization.
* Personalize content. Give frequent illustrations relating to students' and teachers' experiences.
* Emphasize a positive class climate and helpful relationships with others.

Source: Pat Guild (1990), *Using Learning Styles to Help Students Be Successful*, Seattle, Washington: Seattle Public Schools.

brain research folks tend to focus on medical research as the source of their learning theories. Learning styles advocates allude to brain research, but tend to base their position more on psychological research such as the work done by Witkin of *Embedded Figures Test* fame. They cite brain research because it is obviously related more and more to psychological research, but for these people, brain research is not the primary focus.

There are two types of level 1 research on which learning styles is supposedly based. The first is brain research including that conducted by Reuven Feuerstein (a theory of intelligence), Herman Epstein (brain growth spurts, sex differences in hemisphere specialization), and Fox and Wittrock (split brain research, selective attention).

The second type of basic research is the psychological research on individual differences conducted throughout the 20th Century. Carl Jung himself, because of his work on personality types, is cited as one of the pioneers in this area. Witkin's work in the development of the *Embedded Figures Test*, and I.B. Myers and Leslie Briggs' work in the development of their types indicator, has served to operationalize the definition of differences in learning found among human beings.

At a perhaps lesser level, a host of instruments that purport to diagnose learning styles has been developed. The problem with these assessment inventories is that they are plagued by troubles of validity and reliability. In other words, do they really measure what they claim to measure (validity) and are they stable measures of someone's style over time (reliability)? A major problem with the research at this level can be traced to the ambiguity of the meaning of learning style. In fact, a factor analysis of four instruments showed that each instrument was measuring different characteristics (Ferrell (1983)).

Level 2 research on learning styles is actually quite weak. Proponents of learning styles maintain that style-based instruction increases learning. The most far reaching claims appear to be made by Rita Dunn and Marie Carbo, both of whom do research and teach workshops for teachers around the country on the topic of learning styles, and both of whom have materials for teachers and school districts to purchase. Thus they play the dual role of researcher and purveyor of learning styles ideas and materials, something that if it were done in the medical profession would raise the proverbial red flag. But this is, of course, not the medical profession.

Both Dunn and Carbo tout the importance of the actual learning environment, claiming that such variables as temperature, light, body position, etc., should be accommodated to the individual's style. They make further claims about the necessity of matching instructional techniques between teacher and learner. They cite various research studies and sources to support these claims along with anecdotal accounts of great classroom and school success.

Many outside the movement are critical of the research used to support learning styles. The criticisms include the following points:

- The validity and reliability of the instruments are questionable, and that many learning styles theorists have not distinguished the learning styles constructs from intelligence (Curry (1990)).

- The experimental designs employed in classroom-based learning styles research are weak to nonexistent with inadequate controls. Robert Slavin states: "What has never been studied, to my knowledge, is the question of whether teachers who adapt to students' styles get better results than those who don't" (O'Neil (1990)).

- Bias on the part of the researchers, possibly due to "mercenary" interests (Kovale & Forness (1990)) in learning styles results.

- The Hawthorne Effect generated by the enthusiasm of doing something new may explain some of the results.

- "Many studies in the learning styles literature have been conducted by graduate students preparing their Ph.D. theses under the direction of faculty members with a vested interest in substantiating a particular learning styles conceptualization" (Curry (1990)).

We have seen nothing in print to indicate that any large scale program evaluation has been conducted to determine if an inservice program or a district-wide intervention in learning styles changes anything. Yet, without question, learning styles inservices are all the rage.

CONCLUSIONS

The concept of learning styles is appealing. Who wouldn't want to think that every one has equal ability and that it is merely given to each of us in different ways? Howard Gardner's pioneer work in the development of a theory of multiple intelligences offers great hope for education because it gives us a reality base for considering a wide range of behaviors and abilities within the scope of that elusive word "intelligence." But his work could be translated into learning styles applications only tangentially. And who wouldn't want to try to find the best way for a child to learn? We all recognize the bias inherent in a school system where so much of the learning reward structure is devoted to reading print and writing answers. Many of the strategies identified for teaching and learning by learning styles advocates make perfect sense. However, at this point, we feel that the burden is on the learning styles theorists to provide a clearer sense of the beneficial outcomes of a learning-styles based approach before we would suggest that you jump on this bandwagon. Certainly a decision to change methodologies or to do wholesale retraining of teachers based on the research in this area would be a mistake because neither the quantity nor the quality of empirical evidence is there.

REFERENCES

Barbe, W.B., and Swassing, R.H. (1979), *Teaching Through Modality Strengths*, Columbus, OH: Zaner-Bloser, Inc.
Bennett, C.I. (1990), *Comprehensive Multicultural Education: Theory and Practice* (2nd ed.), Boston, Mass.: Allyn and Bacon.

Cornett, C.E. (1983), *What You Should Know About Teaching and Learning Styles*, Bloomington, Indiana: Phi Delta Kappa Educational Foundation.

Curry, L. (1990), "A Critique of the Research on Learning Styles," *Educational Leadership*, 48(2), 50-56.

Dunn, R. (1990), "Rita Dunn Answers Questions on Learning Styles," *Educational Leadership*, 48(2), 15-21.

Dunn, R., Beaudry, J., and Klavas, A. (1989), "Survey of Research on Learning Styles," *Educational Leadership*, 46(6), 50-58.

Ferrell, B.G. (1983), "A Factor Analytic Comparison of Four Learning Styles Instruments," *Journal of Educational Psychology*, 75(1), 33-39.

Guild, P.B., and Garger, S. (1985), *Marching to Different Drummers*, Alexandria, Virginia: Association for Supervision and Curriculum Development.

Gregorc, A.F. (1982), *An Adult's Guide to Style*, Maynard, Mass.: Gabriel Systems, Inc.

Kavale, K.A., and Forness, S.R. (1987), "Substance Over Style: Assessing the Efficacy of Modality Testing and Teaching," *Exceptional Children*, 54(4), 228-239.

Kavale, K.A., and Forness, S.R. (1990). "Substance Over Style: A Rejoinder to Dunn's Animadversions," *Exceptional Children*, 56(4), 357-361.

Keefe, J. (1986), *Profiling and Utilizing Learning Style*, Reston, VA: National Association of Secondary School Principles.

Kolb, D.A. (1985), *The Learning Style Inventory*, Boston, Mass.: McBer & Co.

McCarthy, B. (1987), *The 4MAT System: Teaching to Learning Styles with Right/Left Mode Techniques*, Barrington, IL: Excel, Inc.

Myers, I.B. (1962), *Introduction to Type*, Palo Alto, CA: Consulting Psychologists Press, Inc.

O'Neil, J. (1990), "Findings of Styles Research Murky at Best," *Educational Leadership*, 48(2), 7.

O'Neil, J. (1990), "Making Sense of Style," *Educational Leadership*, 48(2), 4-9.

Snider, V.E. (1990), "What We Know About Learning Styles from Research in Special Education," *Educational Leadership*, 48(2), 53.

Witkin, H., and Goodenough, D. (1981), *Cognitive Styles: Essence and Origins*, New York: International Universities Press Inc.

CHAPTER SEVEN

THE EFFECTIVE SCHOOLS MOVEMENT

"Effective schools research has become one of the most talked about phenomena in education. . . . [I]f a few schools can serve disadvantaged children well, then other schools can, too, if they adopt the practices and characteristics of exemplary schools."

Stephen Miller

"Effective schools is not a sufficiently robust set of principles to make the kinds of policy decisions based on it that many people would like to. . . . [N]o one has yet demonstrated that you can take an ineffective school, force it to comply with those principles and, as a result, create an effective school."

Arthur Wise

"The problem in effective schools research is that very often it's hard to disentangle cause and effect. It's also difficult to determine from the research how you get what it says you ought to have. It's very helpful though, to have the research, even if it's solely descriptive. It's like seeing a beautiful painting: even if you can't do it yourself, it's important to know what it looks like."

Diane Ravitch

The effective schools movement has been around for more than 20 years. It may well have peaked at this point, but it remains prevalent in many states and districts; and it continues to serve as much of the basis for the highly-touted and much-publicized nationwide restructuring efforts. Dissatisfaction with America's schools during the 1970's led to questions about school effectiveness. The questions posed included the following:

- What is an effective school?

- What makes a school ineffective?

- What characteristics do all effective schools share?

- Can those characteristics be developed into a model?

Some educators trace the origins of the effective schools movement to the adverse reactions to James Coleman's book, *Equality of Educational Opportunity* (1966). Coleman had concluded that teachers and their practices, and therefore schools, did not contribute much to student achievement. He suggested that what children bring to school from their homes and families, and what they encountered from other children mattered most. In response to this assertion, school effectiveness studies were launched with the intent of disproving Coleman's assertions.

Pioneer researchers in effective schools maintained that education up to this point (the 1970's) had been dominated for decades by the belief that success or failure in school was attributable to innate characteristics or to the family environment. They claimed that typical explanations of student failure seldom, if ever, took into account teaching or related school factors. By 1977, Brookover and Lezotte had published a paper titled "Changes in School Characteristics Coincident with Changes in Student Achievement," setting the stage for the emergence of the effective schools movement. This was followed by Edmonds' Five Factor Model (*see* Figure 7.1) which was perhaps the earliest list of the common attributes of effective schools.

Over time the movement has evolved into two separate but related lines of pursuit. The first includes the research efforts to identify salient characteristics of effective schools. The second is the attempt to develop models for implementation in less-than-effective schools in order to make them effective. Let's take a look at both efforts.

WHO DEFINES EFFECTIVENESS?

It is important to understand the nature of the effective schools research, how it is conducted, and, of course, how the word "effective" is defined. The earliest efforts resulted in generic lists of a few key qualities that described the more effective schools. Ronald Edmonds described the methodology this way:

> "In methodological terms, the characteristics are a discovery. First you identify schools that produce the outcomes

Figure 7.1.   Characteristics of Effective Schools

Edmonds (1982)	Purkey and Smith (1983)	NWREL (1990)
Five Factor Model	**Organization/ Structure Variables**	**Planning and Learning Goals**
1. The principal's leadership and attention to the quality of instruction.	1. School-site management	1. Everyone emphasizes the importance of learning.
2. A pervasive and broadly understood academic focus.	2. Instructional leadership 3. Staff stability 4. Curriculum articulation and organization	2. The curriculum is based on clear goals and objectives. **School organization and management**
3. An orderly, safe climate conducive to teaching and learning.	5. School-wide staff development 6. Parental involvement and support	1. Students are grouped to promote effective instruction. 2. School time is used for learning.
4. Teacher behaviors that convey the expectation that all students are expected to obtain at least minimum mastery.	7. School-wide recognition of academic success 8. Maximized learning time 9. District support	3. Discipline is firm and consistent. 4. There are pleasant conditions for teaching and learning.
5. The use of measures of pupil achievement as the basis for program evaluation.	**School Culture Variables** 1. Collaborative planning and collegial relationships	**Leadership and School Improvement** 1. Strong leadership guides the instructional program.
	2. Sense of community	2. Administrators and teachers continually strive to improve instructional effectiveness.
	3. Clear goals and high expectations commonly shared	3. Ongoing professional development and collegial learning activities.
	4. Order and discipline	

(Continued)

Figure 7.1. *(Continued)*

Edmonds (1982)	Purkey and Smith (1983)	NWREL (1990)
		Administrator-Teacher-Student Interactions
		1. High expectations for quality instruction.
		2. Incentives and rewards to build motivation.
		Assessment
		1. Learning progress is monitored closely.
		Special Students and Programs
		1. Programs for students at risk.
		Parent and Community Involvement
		1. Parents and community members are invited to become involved.

you're interested in. Then you watch them and try to figure out what makes them different from ineffective schools. Across the broad sweep of the school effectiveness research there is, for example, substantial agreement on the role of leadership. That is not a theory; it is a discovery.

"The same can be said about climate and expectations and the other characteristics. All of them derived from the attempt to find schools that came closest to the standard of effectiveness and then systematically to watch the men and women who were parties to that environment and see what they did that others didn't" (1982a).

So basically what the researchers have done is to define school effectiveness and track down schools that fit the definition. It is no different than if you were to define goodness as something composed of certain positive traits and begin looking for people with those traits who would be, by definition, good. There is nothing wrong with this type of research except that one must learn to recognize its limitations including the fact that cause and effect are, as Diane Ravitch said in one of our opening quotes, entangled.

In the case of effective schools, the so-called dependent variables (or outcomes) that define a school as effective would include high test scores, high attendance and completion rates, etc. Once schools with high test scores, or schools with test scores that exceed normal expectations, are identified, then comes the descriptive work of identifying the day-to-day characteristics of those schools.

In spite of the fact that people are cautioned not to attribute cause and effect, it is very tempting, having found a school or schools with high test scores, to say to others "This is what they do at these schools, you should try it, too." Otherwise, why publish the characteristics? Go back to the beginning of this chapter and read the Stephen Miller quote. Doesn't it read like a cause and effect statement? We think it does.

The lists of the characteristics of effective schools have varied some over the years, but they tend always to include a friendly but businesslike climate in which school time is used for academic learning and discipline is firm and consistent. Administrative leadership, faculty empowerment, and community involvement and support are generally factored in as well. And, of course, the learning goals are clear. One might say this is merely common sense, but to say it is different from documenting it. Figure 7.1 illustrates three lists of effective schools characteristics. The research has been extended into other areas of effectiveness and has become quite extensive (*see* Figure 7.2).

Figure 7.2.   The Northwest Regional Educational Laboratory Effective Schooling Research Base

---

The effective schooling research base identifies schooling practices and characteristics associated with measurable improvements in student achievement and attitudes and excellence in student behavior. These "effective school practices" include elements of schooling associated with a clearly defined curriculum; focused classroom instruction and management; firm, consistent discipline; close monitoring of student performance; and strong instructional leadership.

- **School effects research:** Studies of whole schools undertaken to identify school-wide practices that help students learn.

- **Teacher effects research:** Studies of teachers and students in the classroom to discover effective practices.

- **Research on instructional leadership:** Studies of principals and other building leaders to determine what they do to support teaching and learning.

- **Curriculum alignment research:** Examinations of alternative methods of organizing and managing curriculum to determine effective approaches.

- **Program coupling research:** Inquiries into the interrelationships among practices used at the district, school building and classroom levels.

- **Research on educational change:** Studies to identify conditions and practices that promote significant, durable change in educational programs.

Source: *Effective Schooling Practices: A Research Synthesis 1990 Update* (1990), Portland, Oregon: Northwest Regional Educational Laboratory.

PROGRAM IMPLEMENTATION

With some reservations, the effective schools research has been touted as a "blueprint" for school improvement. And nowhere has this been more the case than with respect to low-achieving, inner-city schools. Proceeding on the theory that what is sauce for the goose is also sauce for the gander, the blueprint has been applied to a whole range of schools from inner-city to wealthy suburban settings. A number of models and programs have been put forward, but Lezotte and Bancroft (1985) have concluded that most have the following common attributes:

- Focus on a single school as the strategic unit for improvement.

- Use a building-based improvement team consisting of teachers and administrators.

- Employ a long-term orientation of three to five years in planning and implementation.

- Organize around the concept of the effective school as reflected in the research.

- Accept certain basic assumptions about schooling, such as the importance of student outcomes, and the primary focus of schooling as that of academic learning.

A number of programs have been developed over the years, one of the more notable being the Onward Toward Excellence (OTE) effective schools model of the Northwest Regional Educational Laboratory in Portland, Oregon. Others worth noting include the work of the National Center for Effective Schools (NCES) in Okemos, Michigan, and Ronald Edmonds' Five Factor Model. Each of these developing groups urges potential consumers of their ideas not to think of the effective schools characteristics as a simple recipe for success.

There are three underlying assumptions on which the various programs are based:

- That the set of identified school characteristics which accompany success (usually defined as high test scores) is somehow causal in nature;

- That a set of school practices believed to bring about learning in one school can bring about learning in other schools; and

- That these important determinants of achievement lie within the control and management of schools.

Now if (and this is a big if) this set of assumptions is accepted, then the effective schools programs appear to rest on a firm foundation.

The effective schools programs are generally represented as procedures for changing how schools do business, that is, how they organize, how they channel interactions, how they diffuse responsibility, on what they focus. A typical program would call for the comparison of a given school against the character-istics of effective schools. Concurrently, the identification of goals consistent with effective schools characteristics would be undertaken. These two acts would establish a baseline for where the school is and where it needs to be. Next would come a plan for the assessment and monitoring of the impact of the changes. Most plans call for a high degree of involvement on the part of faculty and community, invoking one of the shibboleths of our time, site-based management. Obviously, what we have here is a form of restructuring (another current catch word), and many of the effective schools advocates see themselves as leading contributors to the restructuring move-ment.

Thousands of schools have and continue to participate in effective schools projects or school improvement programs. The results, as you might expect, have been mixed. Some, given the operational definition of success (higher test scores), have been successful. The guidelines for successful effective schools program implementation and school change appear in Figure 7.3.

THE RESEARCH BASE FOR THE EFFECTIVE SCHOOLS MOVEMENT

The effective schools movement fits the paradigm described in Chapter Three reasonably well. The basic or pure research was descriptive, exploratory research from which was theorized a causative relationship between certain school characteristics and student achievement. In other words the theory stated that if your school has these characteristics it would predictably be a school where we would find higher test scores. Or put another way, if we discovered that your school has low test scores, the implication is that if you wish to raise them, adopt

Figure 7.3. Characteristics of Successful Implementation of School Improvement Projects

---

• Substantial staff development time must be provided for participating faculties, at least part of this time during the regular teacher workday.

• Faculties engaged in effective schools projects must not wait very long before beginning to address issues involving the improvement of instruction.

• Faculties embarking on effective school projects must avoid getting bogged down in elaborate schemes to train all staff members in the details of a particular instructional technique or approach at the beginning of the project.

• Improvement goals must be sharply focused to avoid overloading teachers and schools.

• Significant technical assistance must be made available to faculties participating in effective schools projects.

• Effective schools programs should be "data-driven" in the sense that appropriate information should be collected and used to guide participants in preparing and carrying out plans for improvement.

• Effective schools projects must avoid reliance on bureaucratic processes that stress forms and checklists, as well as on mandated components rigidly applied in participating schools and classrooms.

• Effective schools projects should seek out and consider using materials, methods, and approaches that have been successful in school and projects elsewhere.

• The success of an effective schools program depends on a judicious mixture of autonomy for participating faculties and control from the central office, a kind of "directed autonomy."

Source: Levine, D.U. (1991), "Creating Effective Schools: Findings and Implications from Research and Practice," *Phi Delta Kappan*, 72 (5), 389–393.

the characteristics of effective schools. So here in one paragraph you have the complete axis from theory to practice.

The level 1 research in effective schools is exploratory, descriptive research. It is done by comparing a school's test scores with its instructional/curricular/leadership characteristics. Patterns emerge clearly separating effective schools from less effective schools. The research base is quite extensive. Purkey and Smith (1982) have described the research as fitting three categories:

- Outliers: The study of highly effective schools and very ineffective schools, schools at the extreme ends of the achievement spectrum.

- Case Studies: The study of schools across the spectrum ofeffectiveness, usually employing qualitative data gathering methods to determine effective practices, *e.g.,* "time on task," etc.

- Program Evaluations: Evaluation of existing programs in schools which prove to be effective.

The results of these many descriptive studies are quite consistent with respect to the identification of characteristics of schools that are effective in achieving high test scores. But criticism of the research set in almost from the start. The criticisms seemed to focus on two concerns: (1) The quality of the research itself, and (2) the inferences and interpretations drawn from the research base.

IT'S A LONG WAY FROM HERE TO THERE

Among the problems associated with the research literature in effective schools are those as basic as the definition itself. A review of the studies has led us to conclude that while there is reasonably clear common core of effective schools characteristics, the definition unravels when one attempts to determine which are truly crucial and which might be tangential. This is not a trivial thing for sincere people who are willing to give their time and energy toward improving their school. Another problem with the research has to do with how generalizable the findings are. Most of the achievement data were derived at the elementary level, mostly from mathematics and reading achievement scores. What the secondary art or history teacher should make of these findings is unclear. Also, should we think that data gathered from schools serving poor, minority populations, as much of it was, has a clear message for other types of schools? To be fair to the researchers, we should say that consumers should make such decisions for themselves.

Perhaps the biggest problem, though, is the fact that the data from effective schools research are primitive. By that we mean that the data were not gathered from controlled research studies which give one the luxury of attributing cause and effect relationships. Rather, these are observational, descriptive studies that give us, at most, correlations. While correlations are interesting, they can also be misleading. We know, for example, that the sale of Kool-Aid correlates highly with incidents of death by drowning. That is, when Kool-Aid sales rise, more people drown in lakes, pools, and streams. The causative agent, however, is neither factor. There simply is no cause and effect relationship. Believe us, if there were, we would be the first to lobby for the ban of Kool-Aid from the supermarket shelves of America. The causative agent sits outside our neat little correlation; it has to do with the mighty engines of the Sun.

The last criticism that we will note has to do with what one does with a list, no matter how good, of effective schools characteristics. How, for example, does a school principal ensure that his/her teachers carry out the practices which are consonant with effective schools? Does a faculty merely agree to do it? What does it mean even if they agree? How do we monitor the practices of professionals to ensure their faithfulness to the program? These aren't the picky questions of a couple of people writing a book on innovations; they are, rather, the practical questions that link reality to research.

At level 2, there isn't much to report. The movement seems to have skipped this level, perhaps because the nature of the research lends itself to more to large scale implementation.

At level 3, the program evaluation research is somewhat confusing and difficult to interpret. Nevertheless, we'll try. Education journals carry numerous articles about effective school programs and the efforts being made to make schools more effective. The quality of the evaluations is largely an unknown entity. Most of the literature documents *how* changes are being implemented and how schools are changing as a result. The information is further confused by the implication that no comparison or control groups exist as points of reference. So descriptive studies abound, and controlled studies are nowhere to be found. This brings us full circle to the cause and effect dilemma.

CONCLUSIONS

This is a highly influential movement that has been around for more than twenty years. Although this is never stated, we see its roots in the efficiency movement which first appeared in American school literature coincident with the rise of industrialism. One could safely exchange the word "efficient" for the word "effective" with little loss of meaning. Its main attraction seems to be the compelling correlation between high test scores (which everybody wants) and certain lists of characteristics.

If you can accept the assumptions that

- the set of school characteristics which correlate with success (high achievement) are causal in nature;
- a set of practices believed to be instrumental in raising test scores in one school can do it in another school; and
- these important characteristics lie within the control and management of schools,

then the effective schools literature makes great good sense.

We think that the information derived from effective schools research is good information, and that it is well worth studying. The alternative is not to know the characteristics of effective schools, and that would leave us all the poorer. And it serves little purpose to blame descriptive research for not delivering to us a neat set of causes and effects. Rather the onus is on consumers to interpret the findings wisely.

REFERENCES

Brandt, R.S. (1982), "Toward More Effective Schools," *Educational Leadership*, 40 (3) (Theme issue).

Brookover, W.B., and Lezotte, L.W. (1977), *Changes in School Characteristics Coincident with Changes in Student Achievement*, East Lansing: Michigan State University, College of Urban Development.

Edmonds, R.R. (1979), "Effective Schools for the Urban Poor," *Educational Leadership*, 37(1), 15-24.

Edmonds, R.R. (1982a), "Programs of School Improvement, *Educational Leadership*, 40(3), 4-11.

Edmonds, R.R. (1982b), "On School Improvement: A Conversation with Ronald Edmonds," *Educational Leadership*, 40(3), 13-15.

Effective Schooling Practices: A Research Synthesis 1990 Update (1990), Portland, Oregon: Northwest Regional Educational Laboratory.

Effective Schooling Practices: A Research Synthesis (1984), Portland, Oregon: Northwest Regional Educational Laboratory.

Finn, C.E., Jr. (1990), "The Biggest Reform of All," *Phi Delta Kappan*, 71(8), 585-592.

Levine, D.U. (1991), "Creating Effective Schools: Findings and Implications from Research and Practice," *Phi Delta Kappan*, 72(5), 389-393.

Lezotte, L.W. (1989), "Base School Improvement on What We Know About Effective Schools," *The American School Board Journal*, 176(8), 18-20

Lezotte, L.W., and Bancroft, B.A. (1985), "Growing Use of the Effective Schools Model for School Improvement," *Educational Leadership*, 42(6), 23-27.

Purkey, S.C., and Smith, M.S.(1983), "Effect Schools: A Review," *The Elementary School Journal*, 83(4), 427-452.

Rosenholtz, S.J. (1985), "Effective Schools: Interpreting the Evidence," *American Journal of Education*, 93(3), 352-388.

Taylor, B.O., and Levine, D.U. (1991), "Effective Schools Projects and School-Based Management," *Phi Delta Kappan*, 72(5), 394-397.

CHAPTER EIGHT

OUTCOME-BASED EDUCATION

"By designing our educational system to achieve clearly defined exit outcomes, we will free ourselves from the traditional rigidity of schools and increase the likelihood that all students will learn."

William Spady

"Educators are often overwhelmed by the number of innovations and strategies being pressed upon them as *the* solution to their problems. And many schools appear to operate like a system of traffic lights in which the traffic engineer solves the problem at each intersection without regard to the problems that this solution creates at the other intersections; the result is a lifetime of continual change without much progress."

Tom Rust Vickery

Many times mastery learning and outcome-based education (OBE) are thought of as synonymous. However, they really are not the same thing. OBE is an overall planning and restructuring process at the macro level of school or district policy; many times it involves mastery learning as a vital component. Mastery learning, as Benjamin Bloom defined it, is a micro level process. One implements it at the classroom level, and it is generally considered a part of the teaching/learning process.

William Spady, of OBE fame, maintains that our current educational paradigm is backwards. He cites custody and the calendar as the decision making forces that drive our system. He writes that "school decision making, curriculum planning, instructional and administrative operations" are all determined by the calendar. School year, semesters, units, credits, class periods, and so forth are the driving forces. Blocks of time have become the way of assessing student success or failure in the system. One could go on: Students must stay in school until they are 16 years old, state laws require a minimum number of days in the school year, a certain number of hours per week in reading and math, etc. This is the stuff of bureaucracy, not the right stuff.

A PRESCRIPTION FOR SCHOOL MALADIES

OBE is proposed by its advocates, and they seem to be growing in number, as a cure for our schools' bureaucratic ills. Spady defines OBE in the following way:

> Outcome Based Education (OBE) means organizing for results: basing what we do instructionally on the outcomes we want to achieve; whether in specific parts of the curriculum or in the schooling process as a whole. (Spady (1988), p. 5.)

The terms, "organizing for results" and "success for all," have emerged as trademarks of the OBE movement, which now has more than 2,000 member schools in its Network for Outcome-Based Schools which was founded in 1980.

Another definition, this one from the Far West Laboratory for Educational Research and Development, states that OBE is "a comprehensive approach to teaching and learning and to instructional management that has its roots in the Mastery Learning and Competency-Based Education movements of the early 1970's." (Murphy (1984).)

Several philosophical premises underlay OBE practice, but four themes are always present. The first theme is that almost all students are capable of achieving excellence in learning the essentials of formal schooling. Teachers and administrators must truly believe this premise in order to make OBE a reality. Even though this first theme seems reasonable enough, in fact most teachers and administrators probably do not believe it. They will, therefore, have to redirect their thinking away from the traditional idea that some are capable of excellence, many of mediocrity, and some of failure.

The second OBE theme is that success influences self-concept; self-concept influences learning and behavior. The implication of this theme is not only that academics and effect are related, but that there is a cause and effect relationship, with academic achievement being the cause and improved self-concept being the effect. And in time, they begin to support each other so that the relationship is reciprocal.

The third theme is that the instructional process can be changed to improved learning. The perceived problem with the instructional process as it presently exists is that objectives and measured outcomes are often unrelated. Therefore, instruction continues apace and tests are given aplenty, but they are essentially unrelated processes which yield unreliable results. Students receive little or no corrective feedback and reinforcement along the way so that they often have a scant idea of how they are doing in any kind of formative sense.

And the fourth theme is that schools can maximize the learning conditions for all students by doing the following:

- Establishing a school climate which continually affirms the worth and diversity of all students;

- Specifying expected learning outcomes;

- Expecting that all students perform at high levels of learning;

- Ensuring that all students experience opportunities for personal success;

- Varying the time for learning according to the needs of each student and the complexity of the task;

- Having staff and students both take responsibility for successful learning outcomes;

- Determining instructional assignments directly through continuous [formative] assessment of student learning;

- Certifying educational progress whenever demonstrated mastery is assessed and validated.

REVERSING THE ORDER OF THINGS

The traditional school-practice paradigm is one of writing objectives for a curriculum which is already in place or which has undergone some degree of modification. OBE turns the paradigm on its head. *See* Figure 8.1 in this regard. Note the near reverse order of things.

In OBE the curriculum and the resulting educational experiences flow from the *outcomes* that you and your colleagues have determined are crucial. This is called the design-down principle by OBE people. That is to say, one begins by thinking about the loftiest outcomes possible long before one specifies the tasks and tests of school life. How that is different from beginning with goal statements as some people have done for years, we aren't sure. Advocates of outcome-based education would answer that although people claim to have begun with goal statements for years, the fact that they seldom questioned the given axioms of school life (time, subject matter, custody, etc.) speaks for itself.

Figure 8.2 illustrates the design-down principle in which one begins with a clarity of focus on desired outcomes which then become the controlling factor in curriculum and instruction decisionmaking. If the outcomes are taken seriously, the thinking goes, then expanded opportunities and support for learning to truly happen must be put into place. This, as you might imagine, opens the door for mastery learning, generally a component of OBE.

Figure 8.1. Two Educational System Paradigms

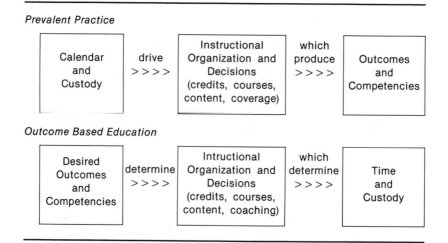

Prevalent Practice

| Calendar and Custody | drive > > > > | Instructional Organization and Decisions (credits, courses, content, coverage) | which produce > > > > | Outcomes and Competencies |

Outcome Based Education

| Desired Outcomes and Competencies | determine > > > > | Intructional Organization and Decisions (credits, courses, content, coaching) | which determine > > > | Time and Custody |

Figure 8.2. Outcome Based Design Sequence and Guiding Principles

---

Exit Outcomes > > > **Program Outcomes** > > > **Course Outcomes** > > > **Unit Outcomes** > > > **Lesson Outcomes**

- **Clarity of focus on outcomes.** Curriculum, instruction and evaluation should all be closely aligned with the desired educational outcomes. Students should always know what learning is expected of them and where they are in relation to the expected outcomes at all times.
- **Design Down from ultimate outcomes.** Curriculum and instructional decisions should be determined by the desired educational outcomes, rather than the other way around.
- **Expanded Opportunity and instructional support.** Content coverage is replaced by instructional coaching to ensure that the content is mastered, using formative evaluation, "second chance" instruction, and continual teacher encouragement and support.
- **High expectations for learning success.** The teachers' underlying philosophy is that all students can learn and expect high quality work from students. Consequently, students may are expected to redo substandard work, take incomplete, and retake tests when necessary.

Source: Spady, W.G. (1988), "Organizing for Results: The Basis of Authentic Restructuring and Reform," *Educational Leadership, 46*(2), p. 7.

Built into the equation as an element of belief or philosophy of OBE is the success principle. The success principle implies that all students can learn and can produce work of good quality, although it may take some students longer or more repeated efforts to do so than others.

UNDERLYING PRINCIPLES

There are three major premises upon which OBE is founded. Those premises are:

- All students can learn and succeed, not necessarily in the same way or at the same rate;

- Success breeds success (just recall the old saying that nothing succeeds like success); and

- Schools control the conditions of success.

A measure of OBE's own success is the set of statements found in the National Goals for America's Schools which demand student outcomes at the center of improvement efforts.

The idea that all students can learn the curriculum traces back to the work of John Carroll who wrote a most intriguing article for *Teachers College Record* in 1963, titled "A Model of School Learning." (Carroll (1963).) Carroll's thesis, which in time was adopted by Benjamin Bloom, was that the issue is not *whether* a student can learn the curriculum, but the length of time it might take the student to learn it. Carroll suggested that we have confused time with ability, unwittingly rewarding those who are able to keep up with the daily flow of events and punishing the slower (not necessarily less intelligent) students.

Thus all, or nearly all, students can learn the third grade mathematics curriculum, for example, but they will naturally learn it at different rates. This ought not to surprise us, but apparently it does given the way school is controlled by time. And that becomes one of the central arguments of OBE: That by reconceptualizing our sense of purpose we are able to determine what we really want to accomplish.

The second premise of OBE, that success breeds success, is something that each of us knows experientially. Some research has shown (Walberg (1984)) that the motivation to learn academic subject matter is primarily the result of prior learning. In other words, the rich get richer and the poor get poorer. OBE enthusiasts point to success for every learner as something that needs to be built into the goal structure. Who could argue?

The third premise of OBE, that schools control the conditions of success, is depressing if one thinks of the realities of school life for many children who walk down a lonely road of failure every day. On the other hand, it is an empowering idea if one thinks of the possibilities. Again, the idea is that by reconceptualizing our very sense of purpose, we will think in terms of success for all rather than in terms of a competitive system where learning is treated as a scarce resource available only to a few.

TRADITIONAL, TRANSITIONAL, TRANSFORMATIONAL OBE

Like all movements, OBE is differentially implemented in real world situations. At present there appear to be three versions of what OBE means to school personnel. The purest form, and the one touted by Spady, is Transformational OBE. As the word transformation implies, this form of OBE calls for a complete restructuring of the schools. Existing curriculum models, instructional systems, and methods of assessment would necessarily be replaced as dictated by the desired outcomes as identified by school personnel. Anything less than this represents compromise with the old ways of doing things, and of course, in such circumstances one always risks the possibility of making great efforts merely to perfect a mistake.

Let us digress into what we hope will be a meaningful example. If a desired outcome of the school experience is that students will think spatially, geometry comes quickly to mind. The reason this is so is because geometry is already in the curriculum and it always has been. But maybe, just maybe, a course in architecture and design would get students to the desired outcome more readily than would geometry. So in a true transformation all bets are off. The existing curriculum must carry a burden of proof against the desired outcomes. It's a rather refreshing idea in many ways.

At the other extreme is the form of OBE called Traditional. It is widely used today. The starting point for school districts using the Traditional form is the existing curriculum. Spady notes that this should more properly be called CBE, or Curriculum-Based Objectives, because the curriculum as it exists dictates the planning process. Here one would ask "How can geometry help our students think spatially?" In one sense, this form serves the role of "straw man" which gets beaten up by the

OBE purists as playing more of a confusing than a clarifying role in educational reform.

In between the two extreme forms one finds Transitional OBE. Whether this form is analogous to the ill-fated attempt to "transition" Americans to the metric system of a few years ago (remember the highway signs that listed both mph and kph?) or whether it is a useful way to wean school systems away from the academic-discipline domination of traditional curriculum to clarifying outcomes in advance is problematic.

IMPLEMENTING OBE

The OBE implementation process begins with a commitment on the part of administrators, teachers, parents, and community to clarifying educational outcomes for students. Here planners are encouraged to think as grandly as possible about the goal structure of education. This stage is crucial because it is here that planners have the opportunity to reinvent the purpose of the school. All subsequent decisions about materials, learning environments, grades, etc., flow from the goal structure for better or for worse.

Once the goal structure is secured, one enters the second stage of OBE, that of aligning the curriculum with a set of objectives. As basic and obvious as this seems, it isn't. This is so because the objectives are at least theoretically freed from the constraints of tradition. So now, having begun anew, we are able to close the gap between what we say will happen and indeed what does happen in classrooms.

Within actual classrooms OBE is tolerant of a variety of teaching/learning strategies, but almost always mastery learning for each student is emphasized. Keep in mind that mastery learning is in fact method neutral. Of course, it is far easier to "prove" mastery on the basis of text, worksheets, etc. than it is to document it where students are doing projects and activities; but that is an age-old problem. Student achievement, however, becomes the determining factor rather than time, schedule, etc.

An evaluation plan, whatever form evaluation takes, must

be developed in such a way that evaluation is aligned with objectives and curriculum. In its extreme form, this involves teaching to the test. But given the alternative, teaching and testing as unrelated entities, it might not be such a bad idea. The point is, that when teaching is aligned with testing, the latter becomes a natural outgrowth of the former. More than anything else, the OBE people have refocused our attention toward the concept of validity in assessment, and this itself is a major contribution.

THE RESEARCH BASE FOR OBE

Actually there is little to nothing to report at the basic or pure research level. OBE makes no direct claims here that we were able to find. We would say, however, and this represents some interpolation and inference building on our part, that the theory of reductionism is at work here. By that we mean that OBE defines success as increased achievement as reflected by higher standardized test scores. Given the OBE operational definition of success, and given that objectives are reduced toward alignment with test content, we can reasonably assume a reductionist world view.

At level 2, or the classroom/school level, mastery learning serves as the linchpin of OBE. There is a considerable body of research to be found here, and it is rather good research. Walberg (1984), Bloom (1984), and others present findings in the forms of individual studies, research reviews, research syntheses, and meta-analyses (Guskey and Pigott (1988); Kulik and Kulik (1986-87); Guskey and Gates (1986); Stallings and Stipek (1986); Walberg (1985)). The consensus is one of efficacious outcomes when it comes to raising test scores. There is a general acceptance among key researchers that mastery works. The only point of dissent is one raised by researcher Robert Slavin (1987). Slavin points out that test score gains were derived from short-term studies. He notes that studies of over four weeks' duration show no educationally significant differences over other approaches. This is a very important consideration because teachers must think long-term if we are to make real improvements in academic outcomes.

At level 3, or the level of actual program evaluation research, we find many stories about schools and whole districts that have been "turned around" by OBE. Given the previously addressed definition of success as improved test scores, we encounter claims from the far-flung outposts of the empire: Johnson City, New York; New Canaan, Connecticut; Red Bank, New Jersey; Sparta, Illinois; and the list goes on. The fact that test scores have improved is a hard fact to walk away from given the manifold woes of American schools.

What is not clear is the quality of these program evaluations. They are largely unpublished and otherwise unavailable for critical review. They could range from those of excellent design and execution to mere "gee whiz" stories. We are unaware of any serious objections to OBE in the literature. Whether critics will emerge with some needed insights to the nature of the program evaluation research remains to be seen.

Still, we remain convinced that much of what is embedded in Outcome Based Education is sound. After all, who could find fault with an attempt to clarify the outcomes we seek? The biggest problem seems to be the tendency to "oversell" OBE. Why not just look at the several simple and reasonable premises upon which OBE is actually founded? And why not expect (and take part in it for that matter) level 2 research to be carried out so that we can gain some useful insights to classroom applications of OBE?

REFERENCES

Block, J.J., Efthim, H.E., and Burns, R.B. (1989), *Building Effective Mastery Learning Schools*, New York: Longman.

Bloom, B.S (1984), "The Search for Methods of Group Instruction as Effective as One-to-One Tutoring," *Educational Leadership*, 41(8), 4-17.

Burns, R., and Squires, D. (1987), "Curriculum Organization in Outcome-Based Education, *The OBE Bulletin*, 3, San Francisco,

CA: Far West Laboratory for Educational Research and Development (ERIC Document Reproduction Service No. ED294313).

Carroll, J.B. (1963), "A Model for School Learning," *Teachers College Record*, *64*, 723-733.

Erickson, W., Valdez, G., and McMillan, W. (1990), *Outcome-Based Education*, St. Paul, Minn.: Minnesota Department of Education.

Guskey, T.R., "Rethinking Mastery Learning Reconsidered," *Review of Educational Research*, *57*(2), 225-229.

Guskey, T.R., and Gates, S.L. (1986), "Synthesis of Research on the Effects of Mastery Learning in Elementary and Secondary Classrooms," *Educational Leadership*, *43*(8), 73-81.

Guskey, T.R., and Pigott, T.D. (1988), "Research on Group-Based Mastery Learning Programs: A Meta-Analysis," *Journal of Educational Research*, *81*(4), 197-216.

Kulik, C.C., and Kulik, J. (1986-87), "Mastery Testing and Student Learning: A Meta-Analysis," *Journal of Educational Technology Systems*, *15*(3), 325-341.

Murphy, C. (Ed.) (1984), "Outcome-Based Instructional Systems: Primer and Practice," *Education Brief*, San Francisco, CA: Far West Laboratory for Educational Research and Development (ERIC Document Reproduction Service No. ED249265).

Network for Outcome-Based Schools, *Outcomes* (quarterly publication of the Network), Johnson City, NY: Johnson City Central Schools.

Rubin, S.E., and Spady, W. (1984), "Achieving Excellence Through Outcome-Based Instructional Delivery," *Educational Leadership*, *41*(8), 37-44.

Slavin, R.E. (1987), "Mastery Learning Reconsidered,"*Review of Educational Research*, *57*(2), 175-213.

Spady, W.G. (1981), *Outcome-Based Instructional Management: A Sociological Perspective*, Washington, DC: National Institute of Education (ERIC Document Reproduction Service No. ED244728).

Spady, W.G. (1988), "Organizing for Results: The Basis of Authentic Restructuring and Reform," *Educational Leadership*, *46*(2), 4-8.

Spady, W.G. (1991), "Beyond Traditional Outcome-Based Education," *Educational Leadership*, *49*(2), 67-72.

Stallings, J., and Stipek, D. (1986), "Research on Early Childhood and Elementary School Teaching Programs," in *Handbook of Research on Teaching*, 3rd ed., edited by M.C. Witrock, New York: Macmillan.

Stephens, G.M., and Herman, J.J. (1984), "Outcome-Based Educational Planning," *Educational Leadership*, *41*(8), 45-47.

Vickery, T.R. (1990), "ODDM: A Workable Model for Total School Improvement," *Educational Leadership*, 47(7), 67-70.

Walberg, H.J. (1984), "Improving the Productivity of America's Schools," *Educational Leadership*, 41(8), 19-27.

Walberg, H. (1985), "Examining the Theory, Practice, and Outcomes of Mastery Learning," in *Improving Student Achievement Through Mastery Learning Programs*, edited by D.U. Levine, San Francisco, CA: Jossey-Bass.

CHAPTER NINE

MASTERY LEARNING

"We believe this solution is relevant at all levels of education including elementary-secondary, college, and even at the graduate and professional school level."

Benjamin Bloom

"This year [1988] marks the 20th birthday of mastery learning. In schooling, concepts that last even a few years are powerful and rare."

James Block

In the previous chapter we referred to John Carroll's article "A Model for School Learning" (Carroll (1963)). It was in that article that Carroll laid the groundwork for mastery learning when he stated that time spent and time needed to learn are keys to achievement. Carroll's point is that given sufficient opportunity to learn (allocated equity instruction time), and time spent actually learning (engaged learning time), the vast majority of students can achieve some specified, expected level of performance.

Benjamin Bloom is credited with implementing the concept by designing an instructional system that has attempted to eliminate connotations of failure by allowing students to successfully acquire skills before moving onto more difficult skills. Mastery learning is distinguished from other approaches by focusing attention on the organization of time and resources to ensure that students are able to master instructional objectives. In the minds of many educators, mastery learning has been associated with increased student achievement.

The theoretical construct on which mastery learning is based is quite simple: All children can learn when they are provided with conditions that are appropriate for their learning. This means that no two persons will necessarily learn something at the same rate. We already know that, but schools seldom take it into account.

REDUCTIONISM AT WORK

Although the antecedent conditions of mastery learning can and have been traced back over the centuries, we prefer to begin our account of it with the work of Ralph Tyler who steadfastly maintained that curriculum should be organized around clearly defined educational objectives the achievement of which can be ascertained through tests which also reflect those objectives (Tyler (1949)). This position makes perfect sense to many, but we should point out that it is an essentialist position premised on the idea of reductionism. Reductionism states that ideas can be reduced to small component parts which can be clearly identified. This premise is at odds with most progressive learning theories which tend to be "wholistic" in nature. Progressives feel that by reducing ideas to component parts certain intangibles are lost in the process. So we have the great philosophical divide over whether the whole is equal to or greater than its separate parts.

At any rate, Tyler's so-called rationale, based on clearly defined and specified objectives, is fundamental to such things as behavioral objectives, lesson plans, teacher monitoring and adjusting, and criterion-based testing. So the process is linear beginning with objectives and ending with assessment. In his classic work *Basic Principles of Curriculum and Instruction*, Tyler proposed four questions that should be addressed by anyone who sets out to plan, develop, and/or implement a curriculum:

- What educational purposes should the school seek to attain?

- What educational experiences can be provided that are likely to attain these purposes?

- How can these educational experiences be effectively organized?

- How can we determine whether these purposes are being attained?

In these four basic questions Tyler addresses purpose, experience, organization, and assessment. Put another way, the questions ask why, what, how, and whether. That's all simple enough and, to quote Abe Lincoln, "People who like that kind of thing find that's just the kind of thing they like." Tyler's is a rational, logical, systematic, linear approach to curriculum building. And this is the basis of mastery learning.

Mastery learning is also deeply invested in behaviorism. All the protocols are there: reinforcement, contingency planning, monitoring, feedback with correctives and adjustments. It is safe to say that mastery learning is teacher-centered in the sense that the teacher directs the flow of learning either in person or through worksheets which are also other-directed. The point is that students do not simply choose what they will do, how and when they will do it, etc. Someone other than the student directs the learning. So, an element of behaviorism, *de facto* programmed learning, is either explicitly or implicitly present. We have heard arguments to the contrary, some of which go so far as to say that mastery learning is method neutral, a point which we made in the previous chapter. But think about it for a minute. How could it be?

IMPLEMENTATION OF MASTERY LEARNING

There are two forms of mastery learning, but they share common elements. One form is called individualized instruction. Individualized instruction is commonly based on the premise of continuous progress (note the linear terminology) where a student works entirely at his/her own rate. Individualized instruction done within the frame of mastery learning involves the establishment of formative evaluation procedures along the way, "mastery criteria" for unit tests, and corrective activities for those learners who fall short of the criterion on the first try. An interesting example of this form is known as the Kellar Plan or Personalized System of Instruction (Simmons (1974)). It is used mainly at the post-secondary level with unit objectives established for a course of study. Tests accompany each unit. Students may take the tests in different but parallel forms as many times as they need to until they achieve mastery or a passing score.

Another example of individualized instruction/mastery learning is used in certain private Christian schools. It is called ACE, or Accelerated Christian Education, a complete K-12 curriculum. In this program students progress on their own through a series of workbooks for each subject in the curriculum. Each unit has a test which a student may take as many times as needed until he/she reaches the mastery criterion which is 80% correct. The role of the teacher is to monitor progress and to lend assistance where it is required. In this program, a student may complete the thirteen years of education in more or less time, depending on his/her ability, motivation, rate of learning, etc.

The second form of mastery learning is called group-based mastery learning. Group-based mastery learning is most closely associated with the work of Benjamin Bloom. Bloom has posed an intriguing learning concept which he calls the "Two Sigma Problem." (Bloom (1984).) He and his associates at the University of Chicago discovered that an average achiever could raise his/her score on criterion measures by two standard deviations (two sigma) if that student were to shift from group learning to tutorial learning. What we are talking about here is moving someone from the 50th percentile to about the 98th percentile which is not a bad move. This felicitous outcome appeared to hold up across subject matter boundaries.

Critics quickly pointed out that, of course, you can raise someone's achievement by giving him/her individual attention as opposed to what happens in a class of 30 or so. But the real question is what happens in a tutorial that brings about the dramatic difference in achievement? The answer to that question might shed some light on how classrooms could be reconfigured to take advantage of the elements of tutorial teaching and learning. One answer could be found in peer teaching. Another could be found in cooperative learning.

But mostly group-based mastery learning has been carried out using something along the lines of Madeline Hunter's (*see* Chapter Two) procedures which involve reducing the learning to manageable unit and daily lesson objectives, teaching to those objectives, formative evaluation activities, reteaching when necessary, and summative assessment. Figure 9.1 illustrates the group-based mastery learning approach. The vast majority of studies point to beneficial outcomes. A few questions have, however, been raised about mastery learning's efficacy over time. We will turn our attention now to the research literature.

Figure 9.1.   Principles and Components of Group-Based Mastery Learning

---

PRINCIPLES:

◆ All students are capable of learning.

◆ Learning can be broken down into its component parts.

◆ Learning must be sequential.

COMPONENTS:

◆ **Planning** — Content or skill to be learned is analyzed and divided into small units with related specific objectives and performance criteria. Pre-instruction assessment identifies instructional starting point.

◆ **Instruction** — Teachers use appropriate strategies based on careful sequencing of the learning. In many instances direct instruction is used involving modeling and practice.

◆ **Formative Evaluation** — Assessment is used frequently throughout the instructional process to determine if the learner is mastering the sequential prerequisite skills.

◆ **Reteaching** — Based on the formative evaluation results, the student is retaught material as needed with new or alternative approaches or examples and with additional practice.

◆ **Final Evaluation** — Assessment to determine the degree to which the new content or skills have been mastered.

THE RESEARCH BASE FOR MASTERY LEARNING

The level 1 foundation of mastery learning is confusing. Everyone from Pestalozzi to Skinner is claimed as a developer of the deep structure. The problem we see here is the confusion that results philosophically when educators think that what they are doing effectively crosses the lines from essentialist orientations to progressive orientations. We would merely suggest that to try both is to obscure a sense of purpose.

The amount of level 2 research on mastery learning is formidable. Only the cooperative learning research base, among those programs we examined, compares favorably with it in quality and volume. The research base extends back over two decades. We will look at the major reviews, syntheses, and meta-analyses.

The earliest synthesis of mastery learning research was conducted by Block and Burns (1976). They found consistently positive results for mastery learning. They also reported that mastery learning improved affective outcomes. Thus students were not merely learning more, they felt better about school and themselves as a result of their experience.

The next review was conducted by Kulik, Kulik, and Cohen (1979). Their review covered 75 studies of Kellar's Personalized System of Instruction (PSI) which we mentioned earlier. They found consistently higher achievement, less variability of achievement, and higher student ratings in college classes where PSI was used.

The most celebrated mastery learning studies were those conducted by Bloom and his associates (1984). We mentioned these studies earlier in this chapter. Bloom's research showed consistent results that group mastery learning produced an effect size of 1.0. This means that the student who is tutored and who will raise his/her achievement 2.0 effect sizes or two standard deviations, will raise his/her achievement one standard deviation above the mean in a group-based mastery learning situation. To raise one's achievement by an effect size of 1.0 represents an incredible outcome, so great that one researcher called group-based mastery learning the educational equivalent of penicillin.

The individual studies and reviews continued apace. Guskey and Gates (1986) found positive effect sizes for students at both elementary and secondary levels. The effect sizes were not as large as those found by Bloom, but were still considered to be educationally significant. And contrary to what one might hypothesize, the most efficacious outcomes were found in language arts and socials rather than where one might expect to find them, in science and mathematics.

Guskey and Pigott (1988) used a much larger data base than those found in past reviews in search of the effects of mastery learning. Again, the results showed that mastery learning yielded consistently positive results with respect to both cognitive and affective outcomes. The findings were consistently positive across subject areas and types of measures used, whether criterion- or norm-referenced. Effect sizes were larger at elementary levels than at secondary or college levels.

Kulik and Kulik (1986-87) examined the research that focused on the effects of mastery testing, a single facet of mastery learning. Of the 49 studies they reviewed, 47 indicated positive effect sizes. They suggested that even though mastery testing is only one part of mastery learning, it could be the most important part in helping to raise student achievement.

Stallings and Stipek (1986) and Walberg (1985) also give mastery learning generally positive reviews and suggest that the research supports its implementation into the school curriculum.

The only cautionary note is that sounded by Slavin (1987). He writes: "I required that the studies had to have taken place over at least four weeks. The studies that produced the big effects—the ones that Bloom talks about and that are cited in a lot of other mastery learning syntheses—were conducted in three days, one week, two weeks, three weeks. Requiring that the treatment had to be in place for at least four weeks brings down the mastery learning studies to a very small number, and I think that even four weeks is really too short" (Brandt (1988), p. 24).

Slavin goes on to point out that in the few mastery learning studies where a genuine control group was in place, the difference in achievement between experimental and control groups was virtually nonexistent. Essentially, he appears to be saying, the studies in mastery learning are lacking in factors effecting external and internal validity. This would seriously damage the exportability of these studies.

Block, Guskey, Bloom, and Walberg have all questioned Slavin's conclusions. Guskey writes, "The results of these best-evidence syntheses . . . are often potentially biased, highly subjective, and likely to be misleading" ((1988), p. 26). Guskey goes on to say that Slavin used an "idiosyncratic approach" to reach his conclusions, and that a considerable body of research shows that mastery learning works regardless of the length of the study. Block, Bloom, and Walberg quite agree.

The level 3 research, or that done at the program evaluation level, is very much intertwined with the OBE program evaluation research covered in the preceding chapter. This is so because all the OBE findings involved mastery learning at the core of the curriculum. As we said, it is mainly anecdotal, and the quality of the research is hardly a known entity.

CONCLUSIONS

The research literature in mastery learning is largely positive. Some of the best known names in educational research circles have weighed in as supporters of this approach to teaching and learning. In spite of Slavin's well-founded concerns, the research in support of mastery learning is about as strong as one can find in the annals of educational investigation. Study after study indicates the superiority of mastery learning over traditional methods in raising test scores.

For those who favor an essentialist approach to education, that is, one that emphasizes direct instruction in basic skills, there appears to be much promise here. If raising test scores is one's goal, mastery learning would seem to be worth serious consideration. And after all, raising test scores is hardly a trivial goal. On the other hand, those who favor a more experiential approach such as that advocated in progressive literature should probably look elsewhere.

REFERENCES

Block, J., and Burns, R. (1976), "Master Learning," in *Review of Research in Education, Vol. 4*, edited by L.S. Shulman, Itasca, IL.: Peacock.

Block, J., Efthim, H., and Burns, R. (1988), *Building Effective Mastery Learning Schools*, New York: Longman.

Bloom, B.S.(1981), *All Our Children Learning: A Primer for Parents, Teachers and Other Educators*, New York: McGraw-Hill.

Bloom, B.S. (1984), "The Search for Methods of Group Instruction as Effective as One-to-One Tutoring," *Educational Leadership, 41*(8), 4-17.

Brandt, R. (1988), "On Research and School Organization: A Conversation with Bob Slavin," *Educational Leadership, 46*(2), 22-29.

Burns, R., and Squires, D. (1987), "Curriculum Organization in Outcome-Based Education," *The OBE Bulletin, 3*, San Francisco, CA: Far West Laboratory for Educational Research and Development (ERIC Document Reproduction Service No. ED294313).

Carroll, J.B. (1963), "A Model for School Learning," *Teachers College Record, 64*, 723-733.

Guskey, T.R. (1988), "Response to Slavin: Who Defines Best?," *Educational Leadership, 46*(2), 26.

Guskey, T.R. (1987), "Rethinking Mastery Learning Reconsidered," *Review of Educational Research, 57*(2), 225-229.

Guskey, T.R., and Gates, S.L. (1986), "Synthesis of Research on the Effects of Mastery Learning in Elementary and Secondary Classrooms," *Educational Leadership, 43*(8), 73-81.

Guskey, T.R., and Pigott, T.D. (1988), "Research on Group-Based Mastery Learning Programs: A Meta-Analysis," *Journal of Educational Research, 81*(4), 197-216.

Kulik, C.C., and Kulik, J. (1986-87), "Mastery Testing and Student Learning: A Meta-Analysis," *Journal of Educational Technology Systems, 15*(3), 325-341.

Kulik, C.C., Kulik, J., and Cohen, A. (1979), "A Meta-Analysis of Outcome Studies of Keller's Personalized System of Instruction," *American Psychologist, 34*(4), 307-318.

Levine, D.U. (1985), *Improving Student Achievement Through Mastery Learning Programs*, San Francisco, CA: Jossey-Bass, 1985.

Murphy, C. (Ed.) (1984), "Outcome-Based Instructional Systems: Primer and Practice," *Education Brief*, San Francisco, CA: Far West Laboratory for Educational Research and Development (ERIC Document Reproduction Service No. ED249265).

Simmons, F. (1974), *PSI, the Keller Plan Handbook: Essays on a Person-alized System of Instruction*, Menlo Park, CA: W.A. Benjamin.

Slavin, R.E. (1987), "Mastery Learning Reconsidered," *Review of Educational Research*, 57(2), 175-213.

Stallings, J., and Stipek, D. (1986), "Research on Early Childhood and Elementary School Teaching Programs," in *Handbook of Research on Teaching*, 3rd ed., edited by M.C. Witrock. New York: Macmillan.

Tyler, R. (1949), *Basic Principles of Curriculum and Instruction*, Chicago: The University of Chicago Press.

Walberg, H. (1985), "Examining the Theory, Practice, and Outcomes of Mastery Learning," in *Improving Student Achievement Through Mastery Learning Programs*, edited by D.U. Levine, San Francisco, CA: Jossey-Bass.

Walberg, H.J. (1984), "Improving the Productivity of America's Schools," *Educational Leadership*, 41(8), 19-27.

CHAPTER TEN

COOPERATIVE LEARNING

"An essential instructional skill that all teachers need is knowing how and when to structure students' learning goals competitively, individualistically, and cooperatively. Each goal structure has its place; an effective teacher will use all three appropriately."

David and Roger Johnson

"The future of cooperative learning is difficult to predict. My hope is that even when cooperative learning is no longer the 'hot new method, schools and teachers will continue to use it as a routine part of instruction. My fear is that cooperative learning will largely disappear as a result of the faddism so common in American Education."

Robert Slavin

"Oh, they had cooperative learning when I was a kid; they just didn't call it that. They called it cheating."

former teacher Arlen King

Cooperative learning is one of the biggest, if not the biggest, educational innovations of our time. It has permeated all levels of teacher training from preservice to inservice. It has been estimated that more that 30,000 teachers and would-be teachers have been trained at the Minneapolis-based Cooperative Learning Center alone. And cooperative learning is not a peculiarly American educational phenomenon. It is touted from Israel to New Zealand, from Sweden to Japan.

The research claims that detail the elements of cooperative learning are more elaborate and documented than those of any other movement in education today. Study after study finds its way into the scholarly journals. Literally hundreds of articles, from research to practice, appear annually on this topic. The major professional subject matter associations have all published special editions showing how cooperative learning can be used in mathematics, social studies, language arts, science, etc.

The claims made for cooperative learning are legendary. Seemingly, it can solve any educational problem. Researcher

Robert Slavin (1989-90), himself a recognized authority in the field of cooperative learning, warns:

> "Another danger inherent in the success of cooperative learning is that the methods will be oversold and under-trained. It is being promoted as an alternative to tracking and within class grouping, as a means of mainstreaming academically handicapped students, as a means of im-proving race relations in desegregated schools, as a solu-tion to the problems of students at risk, as a means of increasing prosocial behavior among children, as well as a method for simply increasing the achievement of all stu-dents. Cooperative learning can in fact accomplish this staggering array of objectives, but not as a result of a single three-hour inservice session" (p. 3).

Of course, Slavin is perfectly correct that a brief introduction to such a complex idea is hardly sufficient to accomplish anything more than a sense of what cooperative learning is. But note his agreement with the wide range of educational problems that cooperative learning can productively address! If it could do half these things, it would be the pedagogical equivalent of a cure for cancer.

What is this apparently wonderful thing called coopera-tive learning? How does it work? Can it really bring about fundamental changes for the better in classroom life? Let's take a closer look at it so that you can begin to decide for yourself.

COOPERATIVE LEARNING MODELS

Cooperative learning takes on many different forms in class-rooms, but they all involve students working in groups or teams to achieve certain educational goals. Beyond the most basic premise of working together, students must also depend on each other, a concept called positive interdependence. From here cooperative learning takes on specific traits advocated differentially by different developers. In some cases, coopera-tive learning is conceived of as a generic strategy that one could use in practically any setting or in any course of study. In other cases, cooperative learning is conceived of as subject-matter specific strategy.

Five or more major models of cooperative learning exist. They have much in common, but the differences among them provide useful distinctions. All five represent training programs for teachers who, having taken the training, should be equipped to implement the various attendant strategies in their classrooms.

David and Roger Johnson of the University of Minnesota are the authors of the Learning Together model. The model is based in a generic group process theory applicable to all disciplines and grade levels. Students are placed in formal or informal base groups which are charged with solving problems, discussing issues, carrying out projects, etc.

The Johnson and Johnson model is built on five elements which trace back to the theories of Morton Deutsch, mentioned in Chapter One. The first element is positive interdependence in which students must believe that they are linked with other students to the point that they cannot succeed unless the other students also succeed. The second element is that of face-to-face interaction in which students must converse with each other, helping one another with the learning tasks, problems, and novel ideas. The third element is individual accountability in which each student must be held accountable for his/her performance with the results given to both the individual and the group. The fourth element is social skills in which students are taught and must use appropriate group interaction skills as part of the learning process. The fifth element is group processing of goal achievement in which student groups must regularly monitor what they are accomplishing and how the group and individuals might function more effectively. Obviously teachers must be trained in these elements, and they must, in turn, be able to teach them to their students.

Robert Slavin of Johns Hopkins University has developed a cooperative learning model called Student Team Learning. His model is less generic than that of the Johnsons. In fact, it has at least four permutations, each of which is specifically designed to address different concerns. For example, his Cooperative Integrated Reading and Composition (CIRC) model is specifically designed for learning reading and writing in grades 3 through 6. His Team Assisted Individualization (TAI) model is designed for mathematics learning in grades 3 through 6. Slavin's approach to cooperative learning represents a sophisticated set of strategies which, as he has stated, cannot be acquired in a three-hour workshop session.

Other notable models include that of Shlomo and Yael Sharan of Israel, which is a general plan for organizing a classroom using a variety of cooperative tactics for different disciplines; that of Spencer Kagan, whose Structural Approach includes such intriguing procedures as Roundrobin, Corners, Numbered Head Together, Roundtable, and Match Mine; and Elliot Aronson's Jigsaw, composed of interdependent learning teams for academic content applicable to various age groups. Figure 10.1 illustrates the several models which we have described in these paragraphs.

Used properly, cooperative learning is designed to supplement and complement direct instruction and the other teaching/learning activities typical of classroom life. Its main function is to replace much of the individual, often competitive, seatwork that so dominates American classrooms. John Goodlad's (1984) research showed that students on average initiate talk only seven minutes per day. In cooperative learning environments, that figure changes dramatically.

It should be noted, as well, that the advocates of cooperative learning are not necessarily opposed to individualistic and competitive learning. Their opposition is to its near complete dominance. Most cooperative learning advocates will say that there is a time and place for each type of learning, but that there must be considerably more cooperative learning in classrooms than is presently the case.

Slavin's perspective is typical of the movement when he states that "cooperative learning methods share the idea that students work together to learn and are responsible for one another's learning as well as their own." (Slavin (1991), p.73.) Slavin's well-stated phrase sums up the essence of cooperative learning. Read it carefully.

Figure 10.1. Cooperative Learning Advocates and Their Models

Researcher/Educator	Model	Focus
David Johnson & Roger Johnson	**Learning Together** • Formal, Informal, and Cooperative Base Groups	Generic group process theory and skills for the teacher for developing a cooperative classroom. Applicable to all levels and disciplines.
Robert Slavin	**Student Team Learning** • Student Teams-Achievement Divisions (STAD) • Teams-Games-Tournament (TGT) • Team Assisted Individualization (TAI) • Cooperative Integrated Reading and Composition (CIRC)	STAD & TGT—general techniques adaptable to most disciplines and grade levels. TAI—specifically for grades 3-6 mathematics. CIRC—specifically for grades 3-6 reading and writing.
Shlomo Sharan & Yael Sharan	**Group Investigation**	A general plan for organizing a classroom using a variety of cooperative strategies for several disciplines.
Spencer Kagan	**Structural Approach** • Roundrobin • Corners • Numbered Heads Together • Roundtable • Match Mine	"Content-free" ways of organizing social interaction in the classroom and for a variety of grade levels.
Elliot Aronson	**Jigsaw**	Interdependent learning teams for academic material which can be broken down into sections; for varying age groups.

THE RESEARCH BASE FOR COOPERATIVE LEARNING

The level 1 research can be traced back to the theories of group dynamics and social interaction developed in the 1930's by pioneer researcher Kurt Lewin. As Slavin notes, "A long tradition of research in social psychology has established that group discussion, particularly when group members must publicly commit themselves, is far more effective at changing individuals' attitudes and behaviors than even the most persuasive lecture." (Slavin (1986), p. 276.)

Lewin's ideas were further refined by the social psychologist Morton Deutsch, who derived a theory of group process based on shared goals and rewards. Deutsch postulated on the basis of his studies that when a group is rewarded on the basis of the behavior of its members, the group members will encourage each other to do whatever helps the group to be rewarded. (Deutsch (1949).)

The work of Lewin, Deutsch, and others led to new perceptions about the power of truly integrated groups to get things done, to sanction and support members, and to provide a whole that is greater than the sum of its parts. It is, of course, in one form or another, an old idea, and to their credit, cooperative learning advocates admit this rather freely. Socrates, for example, used cooperative dialogue between teacher and pupil in order to advance learning. What may have been felt or even known intuitively by some over the centuries (King Arthur's legendary Round Table comes to mind), now had a basis of empirical support. This set the stage for researchers to focus on the efficacy of cooperative group learning in school settings.

At level 2, the sheer amount of empirical evidence which has accumulated from research studies in cooperative learning is staggering. There are literally of hundreds of published individual studies as well as numerous reviews, syntheses, and meta-analyses. There appears to be no review, synthesis, or meta-analysis that concludes that cooperative learning is deficient as a means to raise student achievement. In general, all the conclusions are the same, and all are supportive.

Slavin's synthesis of the research on cooperative learning

(Slavin (1991)) yields four main conclusions each of which is consistent with the pure or basic research and theoretical model derived from Lewin, Deutsch, and others. The conclusions are rather sweeping, but they certainly have a sound empirical foundation:

- For enhancing student achievement, the most successful approaches have incorporated two key elements: Group goals and individual accountability. That is, groups are rewarded based on the individual learning of all group members.

- When group goals and individual accountability are clear, achievement effects of cooperative learning are consistently positive—37 of the 44 experimental/control comparisons of at least four weeks' duration yielded significant positive effects, and none favored traditional methods.

- Positive achievement effects of cooperative learning have been found at about the same degree at all grade levels from 2-12, in all major subjects of the curriculum, and in urban, rural, and suburban schools. Effects are equally positive for high, average, and low achievers.

- Positive effects of cooperative learning have been documented consistently for such diverse outcomes as self-esteem, intergroup relations, acceptance of academically handicapped students, attitudes toward school, and ability to work with others.

At level 3, we find no mention of program evaluation studies that have been done for the large-scale implementation of cooperative learning. The movement has been around long enough that long-term effects at the district level should be available. Perhaps that will become a research focus in time.

CONCLUSIONS

Of all the educational innovations we have reviewed for this book cooperative learning has the best, largest empirical base.

It is not a perfect base and, as Slavin has pointed out (Slavin (1989/1990)), more research is needed at senior high school levels as well as at college and university levels. He also notes that the appropriateness of cooperative learning strategies for the advancement of higher-order conceptual learning is yet to be established firmly.

But we conclude this chapter by saying that for the administrator or teacher who wishes to bring about positive change in more or less a traditional school environment, cooperative learning would seem to be well worth exploring. To do it well takes considerable training and motivation. And to convince parents and other community members that it is more than kids sharing answers with each other will take some doing. These are comments one could make about any innovation, but in this case the innovator will have little trouble finding backup evidence.

REFERENCES

Aronson, E., Blaney, N., Stephan, C., Sikes, J., and Snapp, M. (1978), *The Jigsaw Classroom*, Beverly Hills, CA: Sage.

Deutsch, M. (1949), "A Theory of Cooperation and Competition," *Human Relations*, 2, 129-152.

Johnson, D., and Johnson, R. (1989), *Cooperation and Competition: Theory and Research*, Edina, Minnesota: Interaction Book Company.

Johnson, D., and Johnson, R. (1989), *Leading the Cooperative School*, Edina, Minnesota: Interaction Book Company.

Johnson, D., Johnson, R., and Holubec, E. (1988), *Cooperation in the Classroom*, Edina, Minnesota: Interaction Book Company.

Kagan, S. (1989), *Cooperative Learning Resources for Teachers*, San Juan Capistrano, CA: Resources for Teachers.

Kagan, S. (1989/90), "The Structural Approach to Cooperative Learning," *Educational Leadership*, 47, 4, 12-16.

Lewin, K. (1947), *Field Theory in Social Sciences*, New York: Harper and Row.

Slavin, R. (1991), "Synthesis of Research on Cooperative Learning," *Educational Leadership*, 48, 5, 71-82.

Slavin, R. (1989/90), "Research on Cooperative Learning: Consensus and Controversy," *Educational Leadership*, 47, 4, 52-54.

Slavin, R. (1989/90), "Here to Stay—Or Gone Tomorrow," *Educational Leadership*, 47 (4), 3.

Slavin, R. (1986), *Educational Psychology: Theory into Practice*, Englewood Cliffs, N.J.: Prentice-Hall.

Slavin, R., *et al.*, eds. (1985), *Learning to Cooperate, Cooperating to Learn*, New York: Plenum Press.

CHAPTER ELEVEN

THINKING SKILLS PROGRAMS

"We have a lot of evidence that teaching content alone, and hoping it will cause students to learn to think, doesn't work. The teaching of content alone is not enough."

Arthur Costa

"There is a danger that the teaching of 'thinking skills'—if it survives to become part of mainstream educational practice—may one day become to thinking what diagramming sentences and memorizing rules of grammar too often have become to writing."

John Baer

A lmost all national, state, district, and school lists of goals include something from the grab bag called thinking skills. It's a mixed bag at best, and even for a profession that seems to have little respect for the meaning of words, the terminology is rather loose. The various goals lists employ such terms as critical thinking skills, higher order thinking skills, problem solving skills, strategic reasoning skills, productive thinking skills, etc., all used more or less interchangeably.

The implication of all this is that these "skills" are located at a higher place on some taxonomic register and ought not, therefore, be confused with lower level thinking skills such as remembering or explaining, skills for which, if one can believe the rhetoric, there will be less and less demand as we enter the 21st Century. Before we proceed to look at programs and their effectiveness, let us give you two pieces of advice you never asked for: (1) Be wary of programs that promise to deliver decontextualized "skills" of any kind, and (2) be wary of programs that purport to get students ready for an unknown and infinitely complex future.

THOUGHTS ABOUT THINKING

One would be hard pressed to find someone who thinks that thinking skills are unimportant. This may well be even more the case nowadays as it becomes increasingly obvious to everyone that the knowledge explosion makes it ever more difficult to "master" content. There are, however, several problems which seem to be endemic to the entire area labeled "thinking skills."

For starters, there is little agreement about what thinking skills are. Virtually every program has a list of skills to be developed, but the concepts are quite abstract in many cases with a range of definitions applied to any given thinking skill. For example, "classification" is often identified as an important thinking skill because it is so associated with scientific thought and expression. But what is meant by the term "classification?" Putting things in groups? Organizing whole taxonomies? Recognizing that different attributes lead one to assign something to a particular category? This is very vexing because "classification" is a rather concrete skill compared to, say, "evaluation."

Another problem is that of measuring thinking skills. It is nearly impossible compared to measuring certain physical skills, such as one's ability to pivot one foot while the other foot remains stationary, a skill used by basketball players. We know of no outstanding thinking skills test to which we could refer you. And the several tests that are available have no agreed-on validity if for no other reason than they define the various constructs differentially. /

Whether thinking skills can be taught successfully to students independent of content remains a matter of some debate. Most experts have concluded that they cannot. So the issue of transfer becomes paramount. Can someone who has been taught how to predict use "prediction" as a generic skill applicable to literature, geography, personal problems, etc.? Probably not. And how does one teach others to predict, assuming that we agree on its importance as a thinking skill? Predictions, after all, can be based on evidence as well as on intuition.

Edward de Bono (1983) has suggested that thinking can be

directly taught as a skill or set of skills. His thinking skills program, called CoRT, an acronym for Cognitive Research Trust, emphasizes content-free thinking strategies. An example is the "Plus, Minus, Interesting" (PMI) strategy. Students are given a hypothetical situation and are asked to list as many "pluses," "minuses," or "interestings" as they can about the problem. One of the situations is the question "What if all cars were painted yellow?" According to de Bono, activities like this enable children to use effective thinking strategies which have transfer value to future situations. This assertion has little research support.

Another issue is that of a huge assumption which may in fact not be warranted. That assumption is that teachers themselves possess these various thinking skills. If they do not, how could they possibly teach them? In his book *A Place Called School*, researcher John Goodlad speculates that one reason he never saw teachers teaching concepts could be because they themselves do not think conceptually (Goodlad (1984)). The extent to which teachers have these skills and are prepared to model or teach them is largely unknown. This could well be a fruitful research project for someone to pursue.

Lastly, we know very little about how people think. We know much more about the products of someone's thoughts than we know about how he/she arrives at those products. There is some considerable debate about whether thinking is a conscious or an unconscious process (Baer (1988)). So if we are not sure how people think, how can we proceed with the business of teaching them how to think in such a way that is compatible with given individuals' styles or approaches to situations that demand thinking?

All of this notwithstanding, there seems to be no shortage of people willing to jump into the breech. Programs abound, and the thinking skills movement is going fullforce across the country.

A useful paradigm for considering these matters is offered by Brandt (1984, 1988). He describes teaching *for* thinking as the engagement of content and learning activities and development of language and conceptual abilities through teacher questioning, student-to-student interaction, group discussions, etc. Brandt identifies teaching *about* thinking as encouraging students to be aware of their thinking, reflecting on it, and learning to control it. Students are asked to monitor their own thinking and to make deliberate use of various thinking frames such as those from such programs as Talents Unlimited, CoRT, and Tactics (*see* References). And Brandt suggests that teaching *of* thinking represents the attempt to teach particular mental skills such as summarizing, paraphrasing, and decision making. This last concern is, no doubt, the weakest area, and the one we know least about.

The thinking skills movement is manifest in two forms: (1) The import and adoption of specific curricula or programs (*see* Figure 11.1), and (2) the development and implementation of a matrix of thinking skills throughout the curriculum by a school district or perhaps by a given school. The latter often involves a synthesis or adaptation of one or more of the more popular commercial programs. In either case, the programs tend to focus on the development in learners of thinking processes that are perceived to be lacking or deficient in those learners. Invariably, one finds reference to such "skills" as analysis, synthesis, evaluation, decision-making, creativity, information processing, problem solving, organization, communication, and reasoning. *See* Figure 11.2 for an illustrative example from the program Talents Unlimited.

Most of the programs involve a considerable amount of

Figure 11.1.   Thinking Skills Programs for Schools

Instrument Enrichment
Cognitive Research Trust (CoRT)
Talents Unlimited
Philosophy for Children
Higher Order Thinking Skills (HOTS)
Project Impact
Tactics for Thinking
Structure of Intelligence
Odyssey
Strategic Reasoning

Figure 11.2. A Taxonomy of Thinking Skills

I. Thinking Strategies

Problem Solving
1. Recognize a problem
2. Represent the problem
3. Devise/choose solution plan
4. Execute the plan
5. Evaluate the solution

Decision-Making
1. Define the goal
2. Identify alternatives
3. Analyze alternatives
4. Rank alternatives
5. Judge highest ranked alternatives
6. Choose "best" alternative

Conceptualizing
1. Identify examples
2. Identify common attributes
3. Classify attributes
4. Interrelate categories of attributes
5. Identify additional examples/nonexamples
6. Modify concept attributes/ structure

II. Critical Thinking Skills
1. Distinguishing between verifiable facts and value claims
2. Distinguishing relevant from irrelevant information, claims or reasons
3. Determining the factual accuracy of a statement
4. Determining the credibility of a source
5. Identifying ambiguous claims or arguments
6. Identifying unstated assumptions
7. Detecting bias
8. Identifying logical fallacies
9. Recognizing logical inconsistencies in a line of reasoning
10. Determining the strength of an argument or a claim

III. Information Processing Skills
1. Recall
2. Translation
3. Interpretation
4. Extrapolation
5. Application
6. Analysis (compare, contrast, classify, seriate, etc.)
7. Synthesis
8. Evaluation
9. Reasoning (inferencing): inductive, deductive, analogical

Source: Adapted from Beyer, B.K. (1988), "Developing a Scope and Sequence for Thinking Skills Instruction," *Educational Leadership*, 45 (7), 27.

faculty inservice training. Teachers are acquainted through the inservice offerings with detailed descriptions of the skills to be taught, sample lesson plans, activities, ways to evaluate, etc. Usually, great emphasis is placed upon ways teachers can incorporate the skills to various subject areas and age levels.

PROGRAM IMPLEMENTATION

To give you a clearer picture of what these programs look like we have selected one commercial example and one locally developed example. They are reasonably representative of the range of programs available.

Talents Unlimited

Talents Unlimited was developed in the early 1970's and has been adopted by more than 1500 school districts in 49 states. It is or has been in use in seven different countries. With more than 80 trainers nationwide, Talents Unlimited claims to be one of the most widely disseminated thinking skills program in the country. It is currently disseminated through the U.S. Government's National Diffusion Network.

Talents Unlimited is based on the following assumptions:

"1. People have talents (strengths or preferences) for different thinking processes.

2. Training in the use of these thinking processes can enhance one's potential in various areas of talent and at the same time foster positive feelings about oneself.

3. Training in particular thinking processes can be integrated with knowledge or content in any subject area and can enhance academic achievement.

4. The various thinking processes are also linked to success in the world of work" (Schlichter, et al. (1988), p. 36).

Instruction is focused on 19 thinking skills to be applied to academic content in five "talent" areas. A detailed staff development program is required prior to and concurrent with implementation. The staff development inservice emphasizes understanding the thinking skills and strategies to help the teacher integrate the 19 key skills into the academic curriculum. In addition, the inservice acquaints teachers with lesson materials. Figure 11.3 illustrates the talent areas and corresponding sample teaching strategies.

Figure 11.3. Talents Unlimited's Five Talent Areas and Sample Activities

Talent Area	Sample Activity
1. **Productive Thinking** — to generate many, varied and unusual ideas and then to add on to those ideas to improve them.	In a composition class, students generate a variety of clever ways the element of surprise could be used to create interest in a given story situation.
2. **Communication** — to convey needs, feelings, and ideas effectively to others. The related skills of communication are: description, comparison, empathy, nonverbal communication, and the networking of ideas.	In a biology class students write reports on experiments in varied ways all the statements that could be made on the basis of a completed chart of data on traits observed in sets of cell specimens.
3. **Forecasting** — to look into the future to predict things that might happen or look into the past to consider what might have happened. Forecasting involves predicting both cause and effect relationships.	Students in a business math class are asked to predict the possible consequences if a company did not prepare departmental margin statements.
4. **Decision Making** — to outline, weight, make final judgments, and defend a decision on the many alternatives to a problem.	On the basis of research on various American presidents, students present cases for "the ideal president" using such criteria as education, experience, magnitude of events during presidency, etc.
5. **Planning** — to design a means for implementing an idea by describing what is to be done, identifying the resources needed, outlining a sequence of steps to take, and pinpointing possible problems.	Students who are studying the unusual characteristics of slime mold are asked to design experiments to answer questions they have generated about the behavior of the mold.

Source: Schlichter, C.L., Hobbs, D., and Crump, W.D. (1986), "Extending Talents Unlimited to Secondary Schools," *Educational Leadership, 45 (7),* 36-40.

Writing as a Thinking and Learning Tool

At a local, noncommercial level, the faculty at Bernards High School, Bernardsville, New Jersey, initiated a staff development program called Writing as a Thinking and Learning Tool (Figure 11.4). "With no additional expenditure for materials and no burden of added content for teachers, we designed this program to tackle head-on the task of improving students' critical and creative thinking through writing" (Bland and Koppel (1988), p. 58).

Training for teachers focused on techniques for creating a "thinking environment" in the classroom, the process approach to writing, and strategies for implementing each of the three program components in all subject areas. According to

Figure 11.4.   Bernards High School's Do-It-Yourself Critical
                   Thinking Program

Purposes:

♦ To train any interested teacher of any subject area, grades 7-12, in strategies to improve thinking through the use of writing;

♦ To assist the trained teachers in implementing and refining the strategies through peer coaching and inservice workshops;

♦ To conduct formal and informal evaluation activities to determine the effect of these strategies on the quality of student thinking, both oral and written.

Program Components:

♦ Producing ideas – brainstorming, classifying, prioritizing, inferring, predicting and evaluating. Sample teaching strategies – free association, cubing, mind maps, and clustering.

♦ Expressing ideas – prioritize, classify, elaborate, and connect ideas. Sample teaching strategies – think writing, practice essays, serial writing, oral composing, group essays, conferring and questioning.

♦ Refining expression – the development of a finished product. Sample teaching strategies – checklists, peer conferences, oral reading.

Source: Bland, C., and Koppel, I. (1988), "Writing as a Thinking Tool," *Educational Leadership*, 45 (7), 58-60.

their own evaluation, the project produced the following results:

* Improved student problem solving and clarity of thinking.
* Increased and immediate feedback to students about their thinking.
* Increased participation in sharing ideas and opinions by students.
* Growing student ability to transfer thinking skills from one subject to another.

Most of us would be delighted with such outcomes. We are, however, unsure of exactly how the people at Bernard's were able to document their findings. Just imagine, for starters, the list of variables at stake. Were comparison groups used? To what extent was this already happening as a result of traditional teaching or pupil maturation? These nagging questions are seldom addressed. They get lost in the enthusiasm which accompanies innovation. Nevertheless, we commend them for an attempt at program evaluation, something that rarely happens in any systematic way.

THE RESEARCH BASE FOR THINKING SKILLS PROGRAMS

Can We Get There From Here?

Certain problems seem to be inherent in the research on thinking skills. Any evaluation of the research base must be done with the following things in mind:

* It is difficult to conduct research in an area for which there exists no generally agreed-on set of definitions. Mathematics achievement, by way of contrast, can be operationally defined by a set of constructs, although even this isn't easy to reach total agreement on. Math-

ematics is defined by the various textbooks in use, by the goal structure of the National Council for the Teaching of Mathematics, and by the various standardized tests that are available. One can make no such claims about thinking skills. Remember the Supreme Court Justice who said that while he couldn't define pornography he knew it when he saw it? Let us suppose we could say we know good thinking when we see it. Even if we could say that, it simply isn't enough of a foundation on which to build curricula.

- We are not particularly adept at measuring thinking skills. A few such tests exist, for example, the Cornell Critical Thinking Test. Some IQ and abilities tests contain scales that may be somewhat appropriate to this area, but the "skills" are diverse (*see* Figure 11.1) and difficult to measure and evaluate. We are years away from stable, agreed-on instruments of assessment.

- Given the first two problems, it follows that the means to achieve curriculum alignment seem presently insurmountable. What we are left with, are measurement instruments specific to a given curriculum or local program. These instruments, while often interesting, are plagued by problems of reliability, validity, and subjectivity.

- Thinking skills no doubt develop over a long period of time, and they routinely defy attempts to trace their realization to a specific unit or curriculum experience. As Arthur Costa has noted, "the change in student behavior is bound to be diverse and elusive" (Brandt (1988), p. 11).

- The idea that thinking skills are content-specific and cannot be taught generically must be seriously entertained until such time as it is discredited. We don't think that idea will be discredited. And if this is so, how does one construct content-free tests to measure skills?

Mostly, we are left with observations, impressions, and anecdotal records to document increases in student thinking skills. Any teacher who has ever had to fill out that part of a report card knows what shaky grounds we are on when we give a " + " to Mary for her ability to "solve problems independently." And how many teachers would take either the credit or the blame for the pluses and minuses we marked in the category for the 30 kids in that class?

Basic Research on Thinking

At level 1, one finds a surprisingly small amount of information claimed by thinking skills advocates about basic or pure research in this area. However, it occurs to us that the basic research can be traced to two areas: Brain research and cognitive science.

No doubt we are on the threshold of important knowledge about human brain function. The research referred to in the chapter on brain-based learning is the best we can do for now to give you any insights to this area. Much is at stake here including heredity, nutrition, experience, etc.

The work in cognitive science includes such stage theories as those advanced by Piaget (1970) and Kohlberg (1987), research in information processing such as that done by Robert Sternberg (1990), and research in constructivist thought such as that conducted by Driver (1983). A book well worth reading to acquaint you with these areas is *Cognitive Development Today* by Peter Sutherland (1992).

Perhaps the most relevant of the basic research theories which bear on thinking skills is the work done in information processing (IP). Robert Sternberg is a leading theorist in the IP school of thought. He has synthesized his research-based construct into a theory of intelligence which quantifies IP abilities. By Sternberg's definition, to think productively is to be able to process information effectively. Sternberg's six factors include:

- *Spatial Ability* or the ability to visualize a problem spatially, skills one associates with geometry, geography, architecture, mechanical drawing, art, map making and interpreting, etc.

- *Perceptual Speed* or the ability to grasp a new visual field quickly, something that brings to mind the playing of Nintendo video games, etc.

- *Inductive Reasoning* or the ability to reach conclusions and generalize from evidence or other information.

- *Verbal Comprehension Ability*, or the ability to comprehend text either quickly or at deeper levels.

- *Memory* or the ability to store and retrieve information, ideas, etc.

- *Number Ability* or the ability to manipulate numerical ideas and to learn algorithms.

It should be noted that Sternberg is doubtful that cognitive theories such as his own can necessarily improve teaching. He also addresses the idea of whether thinking skills can be applied generically or whether they are domain-specific. He suggests that people, rather than the skills themselves, are the issue. He proposes that some pupils (as well as teachers!) are domain specific while others are domain general. To the best of our knowledge, this interesting point has completely escaped the builders of thinking skills programs.

Sternberg's pioneering efforts in information processing and a theory of intelligence (1990) emphasizes the thinking processes that may be common to everyone. New perceptions of what intelligence, and therefore thinking skills, means are beginning to emerge from his work. Sternberg has developed what he calls a "triarchic theory of intelligence," that breaks cognitive behavior into thinking, adapting, and problem solving. Thinking, which he calls "componential intelligence," includes planning, performance, and knowledge acquisition. Adapting, which he calls "contextual intelligence," is composed of selecting, reshaping, and maximizing ideas. And problem solving, which he calls, "experiential intelligence," involves insight, automaticity, creativity, and efficiency.

Of course, we would be remiss is we were not to mention the work of Benjamin Bloom whose *Taxonomy of Educational Objectives for the Cognitive Domain* (1956) has influenced the development of more than one lesson plan or district guide over the years. Bloom suggested that a hierarchy of thought exists. At the lower cognitive register are found, in order from low to higher: Knowledge, comprehension, and application. And at the higher cognitive register are found, again in ascending order: analysis, synthesis, and evaluation. These six levels of cognition have been accepted by millions as gospel, and have been used as a template for teacher questions, lesson plan objectives, and anything else related to student thinking. Actually, Bloom's Taxonomy is nothing more than an imaginative theoretical construct which has little empirical foundation. Is it really true, for example, that synthesis requires greater intellectual endeavor than does knowledge? The proof simply isn't there.

Is There Any Evidence?

Given the ambiguities of research at level 1, it is predictable that the research at level 2 is rather weak. We found a number of studies that examined the development of higher order thinking skills (a construct which has not really been established) as educational outcomes, but they are scattered throughout the literature on mastery learning, cooperative learning, outcome-based education, peer coaching, etc., and are not research studies on the programs as we have described them in this chapter.

Norris' (1985) review focused more on the general nature of critical thinking than on any cause and effect relationships and how to develop it. It is, however, a useful review for anyone contemplating curriculum changes in this area. He concluded that we really don't know much about critical thinking and gave only a few tentative conclusions, among them that critical thinking is not widespread and that it is sensitive to context.

At level 3, both the Norris review and a review by Sternberg and Bhana (1986) highlight the problems associated with the research on thinking skills. Sternberg and Bhana's review sought to determine whether these thinking skills programs are "snake oil remedies or miracle cures." They evaluated five programs which had been cited in the annals of program evaluation and found most of the research to be very weak in design and possibly biased. Even setting aside these serious problems, they found the results to be inconclusive and none of the evaluations useful for determining what part of the programs worked and which did not. They concluded "Some thinking skills training programs are probably not a whole lot better than snake oil, but the good ones, although not miracle cures, may improve thinking skills" (p. 67).

Quality evaluation studies are nearly impossible to find. The professional literature, especially that chronicled in *Educational Leadership*, contains many success stories, but few penetrating analyses. The advocates are certainly out there in force. This is a very lucrative inservice and materials area, and it preys on the vulnerability of professionals of good will who so much would like to improve the quality of students' thinking.

CONCLUSIONS

We make no claim that these programs fail to produce thinking skills in students. We just do not have strong evidence that they do. The research in this area is muddled to say the least. We cannot even define or document the existence of thinking skills. Attempts to organize them into hierarchies may bear little resemblance to reality. Most of the evidence in favor of these programs is anecdotal. On the other hand, when one examines the activities and teaching strategies found in most of the programs, they look pretty good.

At this time we would say that the decision to purchase one of these programs and to invest teachers' time in inservice training cannot be made rationally based on the research evidence. Ironically, the pure research base is quite good and is improving almost daily, but the connection between pure research and the work of program builders is primitive. However, if in your professional judgment a particular thinking skills program looks good to you because of the interesting activities and strategies, that may be a logical basis on which to give it a closer look.

In fact, we would go a little further toward a recommendation than our review of the evidence might allow us. There is so much in the way of interesting, intriguing activities in the various thinking skills programs, especially if the activities were undertaken by students in, say, cooperative learning groups, that we would encourage you to review them yourself. Even if the result is not higher test scores, you still may find yourself saying the activities represent time well spent.

REFERENCES

Baer, J. (1988), "Let's Not Handicap Able Thinkers," *Educational Leadership*, 45 (7), 66-72.

Beyer, B.K. (1988), "Developing a Scope and Sequence for Thinking Skills Instruction," *Educational Leadership*, 45 (7), 26-30.

Beyer, B.K. (1988), *Developing a Thinking Skills Program*, Boston: Allyn and Bacon.

Beyer, B.K. (1987), *Practical Strategies for the Teaching of Thinking*, Boston: Allyn and Bacon.

Bland, C., and Koppel, I. (1988), "Writing as a Thinking Tool," *Educational Leadership*, 45 (7), 58-60.

Bloom, B. (Ed.) (1956), *Taxonomy of Educational Objectives*, New York: Longman.

Brandt, R. (1988), "On Teaching Thinking: A Conversation with Art Costa," *Educational Leadership*, 45 (7), 10-13.

Brandt, R. (1984), "Teaching of Thinking, for Thinking about Thinking," *Educational Leadership*, 42, 3.

Costa, A.L. (Ed.) (1985), *Developing Minds: A Resource Book for Teaching Thinking*, Alexandria, Va: Association for Supervision and Curriculum Development.

de Bono, E. (1983), "The Direct Teaching of Thinking as a Skill," *Phi Delta Kappan*, 64 (10), 703-708.

Driver, R. (1983), *Pupil as Scientist?*, London: Open University Press, Milton Keynes.

Gardner, H. (1983), *Frames of Mind*, New York: Basic Books.

Goodlad, J. (1984), *A Place Called School*, New York: McGraw-Hill.

Kohlberg, L. (1987), *Child Psychology and Childhood Education: A Cognitive-Developmental Point of View*, New York: Longman.

Nickerson, R.S., Perkins, D.N., and Smith, E.E. (1985), *The Teaching of Thinking*, Hillsdale, N.J.: Lawrence Erlbaum.

Norris, S.P. (1985), "Synthesis of Research on Critical Thinking," *Educational Leadership, 42* (8), 40-45.

Piaget, J. (1970), *Science of Education and the Psychology of the Child,* New York: Viking Press.

Resnick, L.B. (1987), *Education and Learning to Think,* Washington, DC: Academy Press.

Schlichter, C.L. (1986), "Talents Unlimited: An Inservice Education Model for Teaching Thinking Skills," *Gifted Child Quarterly, 30* (3), 119-123.

Schlichter, C.L., Hobbs, D., and Crump, W.D. (1988), "Extending Talents Unlimited to Secondary Schools," *Educational Leadership, 45* (7), 36-40.

Sternberg, R. (1990), *Metaphos of Mind: Conceptions of the Nature of Intelligence,* New York: Cambridge University Press.

Sternberg, R.J., and Bhana, K. (1986), "Synthesis of Research on the Effectiveness of Intellectual Skills Programs: Snake-oil Remedy or Miracle Cures?," *Educational Leadership, 44* (2), 60-67.

Sutherland, P. (1992), *Cognitive Development Today,* London: Paul Chapman Publishing Limited.

Worsham, A.l.M., and Stockton, A.J. (1986), "A Model for Teaching Thinking Skills: The Inclusion Process," *Phi Delta Kappa Fastback, 236,* Bloomington, Ind.: Phi Delta Kappa.

CHAPTER TWELVE

INTERDISCIPLINARY CURRICULUM

"Many adults today do not understand interdisciplinary curriculum with its child-centered approach to teaching and learning. This doesn't look like 'school' to them. They are unaware of 80 years of research, done in the twentieth century, on how children learn."

Marianne Everett

"Educators should consider integration a potential tool that is feasible and desirable in some situations but not in all."

Jere Brophy and
Janet Alleman

"All things are connected."

Chief Seattle

The nationwide restructuring movement has led schools in a multitude of cases to consider the implementation of interdisciplinary curriculums. The main arguments for interdisciplinary curriculums, or integrated studies as they are sometimes called, are twofold: (1) The knowledge explosion is very real and there is simply too much information to be covered in the curriculum; and (2) most school subjects are taught to students in isolation from other, potentially related, subjects.

By combining subjects around themes or projects, a certain economy is achieved because much of the repetitious material that occurs from subject to subject is eliminated. And when subjects are connected, students begin to see meaningful relationships because the subject matter serves as a vehicle for learning rather than as an end in itself. These are among the primary claims of the advocates of interdisciplinary curriculum.

Among the improvements which supposedly follow suit when a change to interdisciplinary curriculum is made are heightened teacher collaboration, greater student involvement, higher level thinking, better content mastery, real-world applications, and fewer fragmented learning experiences. Most teachers and administrators dream of these outcomes, so the claims tend to be rather attractive.

Integrating curriculum is not a new idea. The learning done in most "natural" situations including apprenticeships, for example, tends to be interdisciplinary. But in school settings, the idea of interdisciplinary learning and teaching came to the fore as part of the Progressive educational movement of the early 20th Century. In ways that modern educators may not even realize, the Progressive movement achieved much in this regard. Language arts and social studies, "subjects" taken for granted in today's elementary curriculum, are themselves interdisciplinary versions of several former separate subjects. And at the secondary level, many districts have for several years integrated their mathematics programs, shucking off the old algebra/geometry/advanced algebra sequence. There are many other examples.

But the current trend goes somewhat further than the prior attempts to coalesce, say, history and the social sciences into something called social studies. The movement today is dedicated to crossing new frontiers between and among school subjects. It should be noted, however, that the philosophical premise remains the same as that advanced during the original Progressive movement. Let's take a moment to examine that premise.

ALL THINGS ARE CONNECTED

"Traditional" school programs tend to be subject centered. That is, the focus in teaching and learning is on school subjects, or academic disciplines. In most cases, those subjects are offered separately, even in elementary classrooms. Each subject has a sequence to it, one that generally becomes more technical and abstract through the succeeding years. Each subject also has a scope within a given grade level. The scope of a subject has to do with how broad or wide ranging the treatment is. The scope and the sequence tend to represent the boundaries of a given subject. But the point is that the focus is always on the subject, its knowledge, skills, etc. The best way to understand the traditional curriculum is to think of its dominant form, the textbook. This is so because most textbooks are written for a particular subject at a particular level.

Interdisciplinary curriculum, on the other hand, takes a quite different approach to teaching and learning. It is far more than a mere blending of separate subjects. It represents a philosophy of student-centered learning. By placing the learner rather than the subject matter at the center, projects and activities take precedence over academic disciplines. This is so because it seems to be the way children and adolescents learn when given a choice. In other words, it is closer to the "natural" way that people learn. The academic disciplines, from such a perspective, are regarded as tools for learning rather than as ends in themselves. If they are tools, then why not blend them wherever it makes sense to do so?

Interdisciplinary programs typically eschew textbook treatments. Thus the curriculum is changed in more ways than one. Most curriculum in American schools are textbook driven. But interdisciplinary curricula focus on group activities and projects, and textbooks, if they are used at all, are relegated to the status of a resource. The curriculum still has to come from somewhere, and if it is not to come from textbooks, what is its source?

The curriculum in interdisciplinary settings tends to be site-based. This is disconcerting to commercial publishers because generic textbooks published for use everywhere are simply not applicable. Interdisciplinary curricula are often tied to local issues, especially when those local issues have global connections. Examples could include studies of local water supplies, wetlands controversies, pollution, etc. Or, equally often, interdisciplinary units will be constructed around a compelling theme, for example, architecture, patterns in nature, the night, cultural heritage, etc.

Teachers and students are involved in the planning and development of the theme or issue chosen for study. Often, a study begins with a brainstorming session where teachers and students construct a "webbing" similar to that shown in Figure 12.1. The webbing, or map, gives structure to the unit while

Figure 12.1.

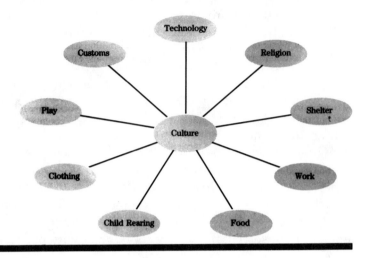

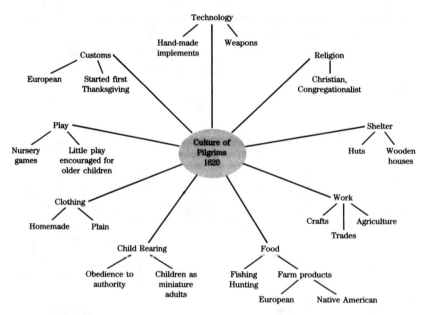

Source: Ellis, A.K. (1991), *Teaching and Learning Elementary Social Studies (4th ed.),* Boston: Allyn and Bacon, Inc., p. 108.

allowing many avenues of individual or group investigation. This stage is very crucial, apparently, because the sense of "ownership" or investiture in the curriculum serves as a motivating force throughout the study. *See* Figure 12.2 for a step-by-step approach to developing an interdisciplinary unit.

A criticism of interdisciplinary curricula is one that is obvious to any essentialist. Because the units are teacher/student developed, they tend to have a seemingly random flavor. The essentialist's need for an orderly scope and sequence is not met to say the least. To interdisciplinary advocates, who tend to be progressives, this is the beauty of such a

Figure 12.2.   A Procedure for Developing Integrated Units of Study

---

• **Step 1 – Selecting an organizing center.** The "organizing center" is the focus of the curriculum development (*i.e.*, theme, topic of study, concept). Once parameters are explored, the topic must be broadened to provide a base for investigation from various points of view in preparation for the next developmental step.

• **Step 2 – Brainstorming associations.** A graphic device (*i.e.*, planning wheel) is useful as teachers and students begin to explore the theme from the perspectives of various discipline fields. The organizing center for the theme is the hub of the wheel; each spoke is a discipline area. The open-ended technique of brainstorming is used to generate spontaneous ideas which will be recorded on the wheel.

• **Step 3 – Establishing guiding questions to serve as a scope and sequence.** This step takes the array of brainstormed associations from the wheel and organizes them. Now the course of study begins to take shape. A framework for the unit of study will develop naturally as scope and sequence guiding questions are developed.

• **Step 4 – Writing activities for implementation.** Guiding inquiry questions have been formulated; now the means for exploring them must be developed. Activity design is crucial because it tells what students will be doing. Bloom's taxonomy is a good guideline for activity design as it will help ensure the cultivation of higher-level thought processes.

Source: Jacobs, H.H. (Ed.) (1989), *Interdisciplinary Curriculum: Design and Implementation*, Alexandria, VA: ASCD, 63-56.

curriculum. It is fair to say, however, that interdisciplinary curricula often tend to favor social studies, language arts, and the arts while slighting mathematics, and this is a serious problem. It is not insoluble, but it is difficult to overcome.

There is also a phenomenon known as "the tyranny of integration." Sometimes teachers become so committed to integrated studies that they find themselves trying to integrate everything they teach. This can quickly lead to a different kind of artificiality. The fact of the matter is that not everything probably can or should be integrated. Matters of discretion become paramount when such factors are weighed. The simple idea that is too easily lost sight of is that integration is a *means* to an end and not an end in itself.

THE RESEARCH BASE FOR THE INTERDISCIPLINARY CURRICULUM

Remember John Dewey?

The primary theoretical basis of interdisciplinary curriculum is found in Progressive educational philosophy. The progressive movement, which included such luminaries as John Dewey, William Kilpatrick, George Counts, and Harold Rugg, reached its zenith earlier in this century. It is a child-centered approach to learning that places great emphasis on creativity, activities, "naturalistic" learning, and, above all, experience.

Progressive education came to be known for what it opposed as much as what it advocated. This was a matter of great concern to Dewey and others. Progressives were opposed to the factory-like efficiency model on which schools depended (and still do). They decried the artificial learning derived from textbooks and written exams. They said that school learning was so unlike the real world that it has little or no meaning to the average child. Robert Hutchins, not a progressive, said it best: "Students resort to the extracurriculum because the curriculum is so stupid."

In his classic work *Interest and Effort in Education*, Dewey wrote eloquently, establishing the thesis of progressivism and therefore of interdisciplinary studies:

> "Our whole policy of compulsory education rises or falls with our ability to make school life an interesting and absorbing experience to the child. In one sense there is no such thing as compulsory education. We can have compulsory physical attendance at school; but education comes only through willing attention to and participation in school activities. It follows that the teacher must select these activities with reference to the child's interests, powers, and capacities. In no other way can she guarantee that the child will be present" (Dewey (1913), p. ix).

The other, more recent pure research basis for interdisciplinary curriculum is found in constructivist theory. As we mentioned in an earlier chapter, constructivism is a theory of learning stating that each person must construct his/her own reality. The constructivity principle states that "construction should always precede analysis" (Post, *et al.* (1992), p. 10). Put another way, this means that experience is the key to meaningful learning, not someone else's experience abstracted and condensed into textbook form, but one's own direct experience. Analysis, or reflective thought, should then follow the experience. So in this sense, the traditional curriculum is not merely turned around, it is stood on its head. Although the work done in constructivist thought is quite recent, it is essentially in harmony with the earlier thinking of the progressives.

Bold Claims — Little Evidence

The level 2 research is close to nil. This may be explained by the observation that interdisciplinary curriculum is itself a large holding company of educational variables that, put together, defies experimental research methods. There would simply be too many variables to control if one set out to do classic, experimental research. This problem, however, has not kept advocates from making wide ranging claims for the effacious outcomes of interdisciplinary curriculum. The following six claims are presented in the name of "research" done in this area. While the claims are interesting and possibly accurate, we feel that they go well beyond any sound empirical base.

- The first claim is that *interdisciplinary curriculum improves higher level thinking skills.* Here the term, "metacurriculum" is invoked. The term metacurriculum refers to the larger, more transcendent ideas that emerge when people focus on problems to be solved rather than on the reductionist, bit-and-pieces activities that occupy so much of school life. The suggestion is that students will become more skilled in flexible thinking as they are placed in learning situations that address connections rather than the kinds of computation, workbook, and seatwork skills of the traditional separate subjects curriculum.

- This leads to the second claim which is that *learning is less fragmented.* Students are provided with a more coherent set of learning experiences and therefore with a more unified sense of process and content. If, for example, a theme such as "patterns in the environment," is selected for study, then the ideas from the various disciplines must "cohere" or integrate because they are merely means to an end rather than ends in themselves.

- Claim number three is that *interdisciplinary curriculum provides real world applications, hence heightening the opportunity for transfer of learning.* It is often the case that interdisciplinary units have real world connections built into them. However, that could be said of units taught within the frame of a separate subject. However, the probability is greater that real world applications will take place in interdisciplinary curriculum settings than in traditional school circumstances. Whether that leads to learning transfer is something we can only speculate on.

- The fourth claim is that *improved mastery of content results from interdisciplinary learning.* The case is made in the literature for better understanding, greater retention, and even academic gains as demonstrated by test scores. Again, the proof is not there.

• Claim number five is that *interdisciplinary learning experiences positively shape a learner's overall approach to knowledge.* The idea is that students will become more proactive and autonomous in their thinking conduct. Related to this is the idea that students improve their moral base by learning to adopt multiple points of view on issues. Again, this is an interesting hypothesis.

• Claim six in the literature is that *motivation to learn is improved in interdisciplinary settings.* Students become engaged in "thoughtful confrontation" with subject matter. More students are reached because of the greater need for different perspectives and learning styles in solving broad-based problems. Teachers themselves become more motivated because teacher-to-teacher contact is enhanced as team efforts are called for in planning, teaching, and evaluating.

All we can say about these claims is that they should be treated as possible hypotheses for some real level 2 research. At present they are nothing more than interesting claims which may or may not hold up under empirical scrutiny.

There appears to be little to nothing at level 3 with one major exception. That exception represents what is generally considered to be the best program evaluation ever conducted. It was called "The Eight Year Study." The purpose of the Eight Year Study (1932-1940) was to determine whether a curriculum designed to meet the needs and interests of students is as effective at preparing students for college as is a traditional, subject-centered program. The study involved 30 progressive or experimental high schools which were matched as closely as possible with traditional comparison schools. Much of the curricular experience in the progressive schools was interdisciplinary in nature. The findings of the studies indicated that students from the progressive schools were as well prepared for college as their traditional counterparts with regard to academics and were more involved in social and extracurricular activities. In spite of the evidence, the study had little real effect on school life, and the weight of tradition prevailed, as it so often does.

We realize that it is stretching things a bit to claim the Eight Year Study as a program evaluation of interdisciplinary curriculum. However, many of the curricular offerings in the progressive schools were what are called "core curriculum" which is a way of combining subjects, say, English and history, into a single offering called "Social Living." In fact, much of middle school philosophy emerged from the progressive movement, and one of the tenets of middle school philosophy is that of interdisciplinary curriculum which focuses on broad themes and issues.

CONCLUSION

The idea of approaching the school curriculum from an interdisciplinary perspective rather than on the basis of separate subjects is a compelling idea. We know that the separating of academic disciplines for scholarly purposes probably makes sense. But for children and adolescents who are still in the process of adapting and organizing their own schema, such an artificial separation probably makes little sense. On the other hand, students readily understand the purpose of a project or an activity based on an interesting theme or issue.

We also know that schools are often a curious place where large numbers of people, students and teachers, congregate but are expected to work separately. Obviously interdisciplinary study is a way of bringing people together. Teachers we have known who have become involved in interdisciplinary teaching have told us that they are really getting to know some of their colleagues for the first time even though they may have worked next door to each other for years. Students, too, because of the project nature of interdisciplinary studies, are given greater opportunity to work with each other. These are no doubt effacious outcomes.

On the other hand, we feel that the claims made in the

name of interdisciplinary curriculum are extravagant and will only raise hopes beyond reasonable expectations. If you decide to approach the curriculum from an interdisciplinary perspective, we recommend that you do so for reasons of collegiality and real world applications. But if you are expecting that such a move will result in higher test scores, we can only say that the proof is not yet there.

And perhaps this is the time and place to say that higher test scores, a very admirable goal, is not alone a sufficient reason for having schools. Both of us have spent a considerable amount of time in Russian schools. There is little doubt that the test scores of Russian students are superior to those of American students. But consider the system they have lived in as a way of life. Higher test scores alone have not improved the quality of life in Russia or the other former Communist countries of Eastern Europe. School is also about citizenship, participation, and decision-making. Please don't misunderstand us: We are not making an argument for ignoring test scores. To do so would be folly. So of course, the best answer is to raise test scores and to meet participatory needs as well. This is this spirit in which we urge you to consider interdisciplinary studies. Professional judgment, whether in education or in some other field, is a difficult, complex enterprise.

REFERENCES

Altshuler, K. (1991), "The Interdisciplinary Classroom," *The Physic's Teacher*, 29(7), 428-429.

Anderson, K. (1991), "Interdisciplinary Inquiry," *School Arts*, 91(3), 4.

Aschbacher, P.R. (1991), "Humanitas: A Thematic Curriculum," *Educational Leadership*, 49(2), 16-19.

Brophy, J., and Alleman, J. (1991), "A Caveat: Curriculum Integration Isn't Always a Good Idea," *Educational Researcher*, 49(2), 66.

Busshman, J.H. (1991), "Reshaping the Secondary Curriculum," *The Clearing House*, 65(2), 83-85.

Dewey, J. (1913), *Interest and Effort in Education*, Boston: Houghton-Mifflin Company.

Everett, M. (1992), "Developmental Interdisciplinary Schools for the Twenty-First Century," *The Education Digest*, 57(7), 57-59.

Jacobs, H.H. (Ed.) (1989), *Interdisciplinary Curriculum: Design and Implementation*, Alexandria, VA: ASCD.

Jacobs, H.H. (1991), "Planning for Curriculum Integration," *Educational Leadership, 49*(2), 27-28.

Spady, W.G., and Marshall, K.J. (1991), "Beyond Traditional Outcome-Based Education," *Educational Leadership, 49*(2), 67-72.

Vars, G. (1991), "Integrated Curriculum in Historical Perspective," *Educational Leadership, 49*(2), 14-15.

CHAPTER THIRTEEN

PERSPECTIVES ON EDUCATIONAL INNOVATION—A CASE STUDY

"To be fond of learning is to be near to knowledge."
Tze-Sze

PROLOGUE

We thought it would be well to conclude this book on research in educational innovation with a case study in the development of a specific curriculum effort. Our focus will be on an experimental development effort sponsored by the National Science Foundation. The project is called Project 2061 and is sponsored by the American Association for the Advancement of Science (AAAS). The purpose of this development effort is to produce curricular models for the science curriculum at levels K to 12. We selected this case study in part because it is a carefully thought out attempt to change the curriculum of the future and because one of the national educational goals of the United States is that American students will be number one in the world in science achievement by the year 2000.

The United States Office of Education and the Educational Testing Service of Princeton, New Jersey, recently released the results of a 20-nation survey of school achievement that showed that while the top American students outperformed the top students of all 20 nations, 90% of American students were below the average of the 20-nation results. Such "good news-bad news" results seem to indicate that while our academic elite is being reasonably well served, students of lesser ability and aptitude are achieving at unacceptably poor levels, a disturbing outcome for a democratic society which can function well only if it has an informed citizenry. This most recent international comparison brings few surprises. Other studies have yielded similar results, leading a growing number of American educational leaders to the conclusion that the next large scale attempt at curriculum reform must be aimed at the great mass of students who are apparently doing rather poorly compared to their counterparts in other nations.

While such a broad based attempt to reform the school curriculum seems the eminently reasonable thing to do, it should be noted for purposes of perspective that the majority of attempts to reform the American school curriculum in the past few decades have in fact been directed at more narrowly conceived, advanced, academic levels rather than at scientific or mathematical literacy for the masses. Of course, this is a point of controversy. Whether it is nobler to aim reform attempts at the elite few who will no doubt provide much of the scientific know-how, etc., in the future, or whether a nation ought to attempt to diffuse its efforts toward broad-based citizen-focused literacy is debatable. Or perhaps a nation can do both. There is no absolute answer to such a question; rather, answers are found in the context of different perspectives on the purpose of public schooling in a democracy.

In the business of curriculum development, the guiding images are typically of (1) an enlightened mind, (2) a productive, contributing citizen, (3) a self-realized individual, and (4) a reconstructed society. These guiding images translate quite readily into the well-known curricular forms of (1) academic rationalism, (2) social efficiency, (3) child-centering, and (4) social reconstructionism. Of course, the alternative images are emphasized differentially from one curriculum construction project to another, and the pure forms are more often than not eclectisized. Experience has shown that to realize all four images equally is extremely difficult and not necessarily desirable, owing to reasons of what to leave in and what to leave out. There is, after all, only so much time available in the school day.

A cursory look at the American school curriculum would lead one to believe that academics (enlightened minds) are the first among equals of the four goals mentioned above. In most instances the building blocks of the curriculum are the time honored academic disciplines taught in universities with concessions to age and ability. Thus the curriculum is composed of mathematics, literature, natural science, social science, and so on. But this is slightly misleading. At the university level, one supposes, literature is taught primarily for academic purposes. But at the public school level, literature, for example, is taught not only for academic purposes but for vocational purposes as well, the reasoning being that people must learn to read in order to compete successfully in a global, information processing job market. And while literature is being taught, the teacher is also concerned with proper discipline, fairness, cooperation, etc., which one could infer is related to citizenship as a curricular goal. And many teachers of literature in public schools sincerely hope that their students will find some measure of self-reflection or personal insight in the great works of literature; that, after all, is certainly possible, and one ought to hope for it. Therefore, all four images are sought after to some degree in whatever is taught in the school curriculum. And this is particularly a point of concern in the broad education of the masses, most of whom will not continue their formal education beyond public school.

SCIENCE FOR ALL AMERICANS

Project 2061

With these thoughts in mind, we wish to bring to your attention a large-scale curriculum reform project, now under way in the United States, called Project 2061: SCIENCE FOR ALL AMERICANS (SFAA). SFAA is an experimental curriculum project funded by the American Association for the Advancement of Science (AAAS) and the National Science

Foundation (NSF). Planning for the project began in 1986, the year in which Comet Halley reappeared in our skies. Comet Halley will reappear in 2061, and that is the significance of the project title. The development phase will continue throughout this decade. The purpose of the project is simple: TO RAISE THE LEVEL OF SCIENTIFIC LITERACY OF ALL AMERI-CANS. Scientific literacy is presumed by the project's authors to include the natural sciences, technology, and mathematics, with connections to the social sciences, the humanities, and other parts of the school curriculum. The project is directed by Professor F. James Rutherford, formerly of the Harvard Physics Project, and currently the chief school officer of the National Science Foundation. The associate project directors are Professor Andrew Ahlgren of the University of Minnesota and Professor Joellen Roseman, formerly a professor of biochemistry at Johns Hopkins University. A book written by Rutherford and Ahlgren, titled *Science for All Americans*, describes the goal structure and scope of the project. It was published by Oxford University Press in 1991.

The project is ambitious in its vision of curriculum reform, seeking to set aside all preconceived notions of what is or is not possible in school settings. Such conventional ideas of school propriety as age- or grade-level grouping of students, the integrity of separate academic disciplines set apart from each other, learning as something that takes place exclusively on the school grounds, etc., are routinely challenged by the project's architects. But the purpose of the project is clear: The extension of scientific literacy to all students.

To achieve this purpose, teacher teams from six sites (San Diego and San Francisco in California; San Antonio, Texas; Philadelphia, Pennsylvania; Athens, Georgia; and Macfarland, Wisconsin) around the country have been assembled and brought together to work with a variety of scientists, learning theorists, and curriculum specialists in order to construct prototype learning materials. At the present time, each site team has developed a curriculum model designed to meet the 13 specific goals of the project. (*See* Figure 13.1 for a list of the specific project goals.) Each of the teacher-developed, consultant-assisted models is somewhat different owing to reasons

Figure 13.1. Goals of Science for All Americans

+ **Nature of Science:** The scientific world view; scientific inquiry; the scientific enterprise.

+ **The Nature of Mathematics:** Features of mathematics; mathematical processes.

+ **The Nature of Technology:** Science and technology; principles of technology; technology and society.

+ **The Physical Setting:** The universe; the Earth; forces that shape the Earth; the structure of matter; transformations of energy; the motion of things; the forces of nature.

+ **The Living Environment:** Diversity of life; heredity; cells; interdependence of life; flow of matter and energy; evolution of life.

+ **The Human Organism:** Human identity; life cycle; basic functions; learning; physical health; mental health.

+ **Human Society:** Cultural effects on behavior; group organization and behavior; social change; social tradeoffs; forms of political and economic organization; social conflict; worldwide social systems.

+ **The Designed World:** The human presence; agriculture; materials; manufacturing; energy sources; energy use; communication; information processing; health technology.

+ **The Mathematical World:** Numbers; symbolic relationships; shapes; uncertainty; summarizing data; sampling; reasoning.

+ **Historical Perspectives:** Displacing the Earth from the center of the universe; uniting the heavens and Earth; uniting matter and energy, time and space; extending time; setting the Earth's surface in motion; understanding fire; splitting the atom; explaining the diversity of life; discovering germs; handselling power.

+ **Common Themes:** Systems; models; constancy; patterns of change; evolution; scale.

+ **Habits of Mind:** Values and attitudes; skills.

Source: *Science for All Americans* (1991), Oxford University Press.

of team composition, geographic/cultural factors, and to the instructions given to each team from the project directors.

In the United States there has been a history of government-funded experimental science and mathematics projects since 1957 when the USSR shocked the United States by launching

Sputnik, the first artificial earth-orbiting satellite. More recently, the sense of urgency to improve our mathematics and science programs has been brought about by the rise of Japanese technology and by that country's increasing dominance in electronics and automobile manufacture. One of the concerns of SFAA is that this current attempt at curriculum reform must be implemented on a broad scale because almost all of the attempts at reform since 1957 have seemingly failed to have much, if any, lasting impact. Curriculum reformers who ignore the lessons of the past must do so at their peril, and the reasons for the failure of past reform attempts is clear:

- The majority of reform attempts were aimed at a single curriculum subject and therefore were not necessarily compatible with the curriculum as a whole. In some cases the contents or methods of a particular reform effort that addressed the science curriculum, for example, were in fact systemically different from the other subjects in the existing curriculum.

- Most of the reform attempts were thought out and directed by university professors who assumed they knew what the public schools needed. The failure to include school personnel in the planning and development of reform efforts was not merely a political mistake—it also often over- or underestimated the realities of school and community life in America.

- Most of the reform attempts had little or no sustained teacher retraining component, so even if they were good, teachers did not know how to implement them. This was a source of frustration for both developers and for school personnel. Some projects were never given a fair chance to succeed simply because teachers did not know how to implement them, and they therefore scorned or simply ignored them as the work of "ivory tower" professors.

- Commercially-published textbooks dominate the American school curriculum, and it is difficult for inquiry-oriented and activity-oriented projects (which almost of the reform efforts tend to be) to displace them. It is true that a few projects (most notably the Biological Science Curriculum Study) did find their way into textbook form; and in terms of staying power and influence, these were the most successful. But most innovators feel that textbooks at best can only be adjuncts to truly lively courses of study, so the inertia of the textbook-centered school curriculum remains a very real obstacle for reformers.

* None of the reform attempts made provision for the ongoing publicity necessary for them to remain in the public's awareness. Consequently, they quickly faded from consciousness. In a capitalistic, market-driven society even the public school curriculum is subject to influence from advertising, "free" promotions, and other such means of exerting influence on would be purchasers. Most of the experimental, government-sponsored projects apparently assumed that if their product and ideas were good, the schools would clamor to get hold of them, an extremely naive sense of buying and selling in our sophisticated commercial society. School personnel probably never even knew of the existence of many curriculum projects.

* Few of the reform attempts took into account the needs and interests of average students; rather they were aimed at the intellectual elite. The first widespread attempt to reform the American school curriculum occurred in the 1890's when the Committee of Ten, chaired by Harvard President Charles Eliot, argued forcefully and successfully that the public school curriculum should be a simplified version of the curriculum of higher education. In one form or another, almost all the reform projects of the post-Sputnik era followed suit, looking to the universities for guidance in curriculum revision. Many good things could be said about this approach to thinking about the school curriculum, but it is problematic to curriculum improvement that univer-

sity professors, usually the key players, think and act in academic environments far removed from the common school settings to which their reform efforts are directed.

• Little effort was made by reformers to study past attempts at reform with an eye to collecting the good ideas which may have been embedded in them. One way to appeal for funds to support new curricular efforts is to be clear about how new research in learning, etc., has changed the basis for curriculum development. The implication is that past attempts, no matter how well intentioned, were hampered by a lack of knowledge now available. This attitude has led to a disdain for past efforts as a whole rather than to an attitude which says "Let's take a look at what was good about some particular project from the past." Therefore, little real progress has been made simply because so much time gets spent reinventing the wheel.

These are mistakes which Science for All Americans: Project 2061 seeks to avoid. From what we have seen, the several SFAA curriculum models which have been developed at this point reflect an attempt to realize the images of the enlightened mind, the productive citizen, the self-realized individual, and a reconstructed society in varying degree. It should be noted that the various curricular models developed by participants in the SFAA project are more alike than different (our analysis of the models indicates about 80% common ground, and the common ground is found in their experiential focus). It is the 20% difference that makes them so interesting because the differences represent alternative possibilities for the achievement of scientific literacy. And we know that in the course of solving real problems, there is seldom merely one right approach.

The four model types developed by SFAA are explained in the following extended quote from a working document titled "Current Thinking about Curriculum Models" (SFAA, Project 2061 working document, 1992):

"We have identified four model types: Inquiry, Design, Perspectives, and Insight. Each type exemplifies a different way that literate people use science, mathematics, and technology: *Inquiry* emphasizes the use of science, mathematics, and technology to find things out; *Design*, to make things better; *Perspectives*, to inform decisions; and *Insight*, to explain how the world works. (All of these are different from the emphasis today—to prepare to become scientists, or more concretely, to get ready for the next course.)

"INQUIRY blocks seek to answer questions like 'how do we know how . . .' or 'how did scientists come to understand how. . . .' They involve students in investigations, either conducting their own or studying those of others. Closure and student satisfaction come at the end of the investigation with an answer to the question to the question (an/or improving the question). Students will understand better how science is used to find things out. Participation in the process can also lead to a more sophisticated understanding of the strengths and limits of scientific knowledge.

"DESIGN blocks begin with a problem, need, or opportunity and involve students in planning, implementing, and evaluating design solutions. The designs they study may be either their own or those of others—or 'designs' found in nature. Closure and student satisfaction come from having figured out a solution or making something better (or at least figuring out what went wrong). They can understand better how science, mathematics, and technology play roles in design and the tradeoffs involved. And they should be better able to analyze and compare—even troubleshoot—products and systems.

"PERSPECTIVES begin with a societal issue. Students consider alternative lines of action, drawing on science, mathematics, and technology to inform their thinking. Students may act on their decisions or make recommendations to others. Closure and student satisfaction come when a decision is made or an action is recommended or taken. Students will understand better the decision-making process, appreciate that costs and benefits must be weighed, fact and opinion can be mixed, information can be distorted, and conclusions can be drawn without considering alternatives.

"INSIGHT blocks start with a phenomenon to be explored. Students ask 'What causes this to happen?' or 'What happens when. . . ?' They study and apply scientific concepts and theories, seeing which are helpful and which not. Closure and student satisfaction come from understanding something better and being able to use the explanation in a new context. Insight blocks are most are most similar to what may purport to occur in schools now – but when done well."

Each model reflects, to some degree, a vision of openness, informality, creativity, choices, exploration, and reflective thinking by teachers and students. Each model questions the wisdom of textbook dependence, passive learning, centralized authority, age-determined grouping, and uniform, depersonalized learning environments.

Drawn back to the corners, the models portray, approximately, the time-honored dimensions of curricular thought: (1) academic rationalism, (2) social efficiency, (3) child-centering, and (4) social reconstructionism. The SFAA models are not easily categorized along these lines simply because each reflects the seemingly natural inclination of the practitioners who developed them to be eclectic rather pure in their thinking. Still it is useful to attempt to portray the various camps in as sharp relief as possible. Taken to extremes, the points of view become caricaturized and are clearly outrageous, so we are doing this purely for the purposes of analysis. We suppose that an observer who saw the models in action in classrooms might have some difficulty knowing which was which.

In its purest form the ACADEMIC RATIONALIST curriculum is designed to enlighten students with scholarly knowledge, insights, and values. Teaching the canons of scientific thought and inquiry to the young serves to preserve and protect the various scholarly disciplines, and such practice serves to ensure the continued expansion of knowledge as each succeeding generation becomes enlightened. It can be argued that academic knowledge needs no defense as curriculum content. It has its own intrinsic value. The ideal teaching form is that of mentor and pupils engaged in investigations which enable the young to temper with inductive learning that which they receive in more traditional, didactic form from scholarly teachers. What has become increasingly problematic in recent times is how anyone can presume to determine what narrow slices of academic knowledge are to be parceled out in what scope and sequence over the school years, and that is used as an argument for inquiry learning as a way for the young to perceive the process of knowledge development as opposed to receiving nothing more than the products of someone else's scientific research. The English philosopher Herbert Spencer's question "What knowledge is of most worth?" is certainly a more difficult curricular question now than it was when he posed it in the 19th Century. In any event, an SFAA curriculum model titled, INQUIRY, has emerged, and it basically fits the description given above, with a bit of tempering from society-linked issues and personal choice by students.

SOCIAL EFFICIENCY as a guide to curriculum content is premised on the view that the schools are the training grounds for the development of future citizens who must be economically productive and who should play socially redeeming roles in society. It is clear that practical life skills are the keys to the school experience. The scholarly disciplines are useful to the extent that they furnish much the information necessary to move society forward. They are, therefore, tools to be used in the design of an improved society. Academic knowledge is not an end in itself. Academic knowledge need not be purveyed in pure forms. Utilitarian function can as well form the basis of the curriculum. In fact, one could well argue that technology, rather than academic science, is for most children a more reasonable basis on which to build a curriculum. What is difficult to come to terms with is how curriculum developers can create materials and experiences that will address the societal needs of an uncharted future. And to what extent ought the purpose of school be to value individuals in terms of their potential to contribute to the state? This, in admittedly more extreme forms is what education is all about in totalitarian nations.

The CHILD-CENTERED approach focuses on the needs and the growth and development of the individual as the key to the curriculum. The premise is that true learning is spontaneous, emotionally-invested, and cannot be prepackaged. Too much time is spent in school learning someone else's knowledge resulting in several serious deficiencies: Lack of self-understanding because of the school's failure to focus on the individual; lack of interest because of artificial learning experiences; and lack of meaning because of factory-like environments. The Roman orator Quintilian introduced the doctrine of interest in the First Century A.D., so it is hardly a new idea that people learn best when they can decide what to learn for themselves. Exploration, investigation, choosing what to learn, etc., represent the encounters that set the young on the path to meaningful learning. The problem is found in the romantic presumption that children really want to learn something worthwhile in spite of so much evidence to the contrary. Also, there is the unwillingness of many teachers to give up the spotlight. They love to stand in front of the class lecturing or asking questions, etc. And, of course, there is the fear that crazy-quilt patterns of knowledge will emerge when no one claims to have put together a systematic scope and sequence of the crucial material that all must learn.

SOCIAL RECONSTRUCTIONISM promises a better world through the school-based efforts of a coming generation, a generation that does not carry the "baggage" of its forebears. Youth is a time of idealism, a time when people are willing to try to make a difference in the world. The vision of an improved social fabric, of reform where injustice, inequality, and apathy prevail, is certainly a compelling premise on which to build a curriculum. Knowledge, skills, and group effort can be brought to bear to begin the creation of a world where people care about one another, the environment, the fair distribution of wealth, the acceptance of diversity, and a world at peace. The social activism and sense of engagement in the real world that flow from this approach brings meaning to learning. Students begin to perceive knowledge as power to effect positive change. The difficulty here is found in the naive thinking that schools can be the fulcrums for change in a world of more real, more powerful social forces, and in the manipulative perception that childhood should be managed in such fashion as to meet the needs of a few well-intentioned adults who want another chance to change the world. Like its cousin, the child-centered curriculum, the social reconstructionist curriculum is subject to similar criticisms of unpredictable content coverage and poor choices by teachers and students of what to study.

The SFAA models are not so clear cut as to be placed neatly within any of the preceding categories. The categories do, nevertheless, capture the range of the SFAA models. Each model fits more or less in one or more of the categories, although the extent to which that is true might cause some debate. Beyond that, each model has a variously explicit/ implicit Experiential premise, and each model appears to share the following elements of a curricular world view:

- THE SCHOOL CURRICULUM AND THE SEARCH FOR MEANING. We cannot afford to presume that traditional forms of the curriculum are personally, societally, or even academically meaningful as we make the very difficult global transition into an information age.

- MORAL IMPERATIVES IN A FREE SOCIETY. Human beings expect to be invested in the most fundamental processes of life, and they have a desire to extend that investment to others. Therefore, freedom, duty, compassion, and justice must be experienced at school if the curriculum is to be based in the values of a democratic society.

- THE TRANSITION FROM TEACHING TO LEARNING. The standardized, centralized, synchronized industrial model of school with all its factory-like metaphors must be abandoned. The assumption that the narrow specialization of subjects and teachers is the best path to learning must be questioned. A new model must be developed which supports learners in their personal quest toward intellectual, moral, and spiritual reality.

- MAKING CONNECTIONS AND EXPLORING RELA-
  TIONSHIPS. Students are traditionally given information and skills from discrete disciplines and are expected, apparently, to provide their own connections. A
  curriculum that invites connections, that allows students
  to explore the relationship of ideas across disciplinary
  lines, and that builds in time for reflective thought is a
  curriculum whose time has come.

- THE NATURE OF KNOWLEDGE. Given the exponen-
  tial growth of information and knowledge which continues unabated, schools must ask, with T.S. Eliot,
  whether all the knowledge is to be lost in information
  and all the wisdom lost in knowledge. The search for
  what someone must "know" in order to be successful
  grows increasingly problematic. The challenge is to
  select that knowledge for consumption that is of lasting
  value.

Our attempt to examine the curricular ideology of the
various SFAA models leaves us with the following conclusions
about this most current case study in American school curriculum reform:

- Each of the participant-designed models has the potential for achieving the SFAA goals. Only time will tell if
  some of them are more clearly aimed at the SFAA goal
  structure than others.

- Each of the models clearly has a concomitant goal
  structure, one that exists outside the stated goals of
  SFAA. The mainly cognitive goal structure of SFAA
  appears to be supplemented in the rhetoric of the
  various models with statements of personalization, *esprit
  de corps*, and community in growth and development.

- The commonalities expressed in the models are indica-
  tive of the consensus of the value of Experiential
  learning in school environments.

- None of the models are presented as radical attempts to reform the curriculum. They fall, rather, within the scope of the progressive/cognitive reform attempts made at various times throughout this century. The lessons of the past show us the failure of abrupt, revolutionary attempts to change the schools because the schools are by nature conserving institutions which will tolerate only a certain degree of discontinuity with their complex, labyrinthine systems.

CONCLUSION

Curriculum reform is a never-ending quest in a democratic society. The multiple perspectives that are allowed, indeed invited, to exist in an open society will invariably seek attention in a setting as important as the public schools. Therefore, reform must be viewed as a process rather than as an end result. The citizens of a democracy simply cannot afford to become complacent about any of their cherished institutions of government, the courts, the workplace, church, social organizations, and especially, the schools. Ongoing attempts at reform provide a sense of vitality and continued renewal that is lacking in static environments. This spirit of renewal is surely what Thomas Jefferson had in mind when he encouraged each generation to examine and reexamine its institutions to the point, if necessary, of revolution.

EPILOGUE

Have not the verses of Homer continued twenty-five hundred years or more without the loss of a syllable or letter; during which time infinite palaces, temples, castles, cities have been decayed and demolished.

Francis Bacon

The spirit of educational reform is endowed with perennial qualities. There seems to be a neverending quest by educators for better programs, better delivery systems, better ideas about how students learn. Each year new approaches are touted, and thousands of teachers and administrators find themselves in meetings, taking notes while listening to some guru who claims to have at last gotten to the heart of the matter. The claims themselves have an enduring nature; only topics change.

Few fields of endeavor are as vulnerable as ours is to miracle cures. After all, we want desperately to be efficient, to provide equality of opportunity for children, and to promote excellence. We want our schools to be places of good repute. Each of us wants people to talk about our own school with a sense of admiration. We want our students to recall their days with us as times of hope and glory. And why not? Why expect less of ourselves?

Those teachers and administrators who have toiled in the vineyards of education over time come to know the rhythms of the school year. The hope and the high expectations of a golden

September morning when the whole year lies before us and even the most mediocre student in the most mediocre class taught by the most mediocre teacher seems filled with the promise of success. The ambiguities of a cold and dark January late afternoon when the kids have left for the day and you're sitting at your desk wondering what's the point and why I am doing this? And that day in June, when it's over once more and you made it, and so did the kids, and you're not sure how, and they're saying goodbye to you ,and where did the year go anyway? And that kid comes up to say goodbye, the one that everybody but you had written off, and he hands you a note that simply says "Thank you for caring so much."

Maybe there is something more to teaching and learning than the quest for the latest program. Maybe it has more to do with a caring teacher and a group of kids who want to learn something than we are willing to admit in this age of "scientific" advances. Still we look for help because it's a tough job and we want to do it right. How do we know whether to invest our time, our energy, the public's money, and the other resources that it takes to innovate?

THE GRAVEYARD OF LOST SHIPS

To paraphrase singer Neil Diamond, there is no way to count or to measure the cost of the energy lost in the annals of educational innovation. Today's flagship is often tomorrow's abandoned shipwreck. There was the hot new program that everyone talked about, and if you weren't up to speed, well. . . . Now the same people who touted it can barely remember it. Where are they now? All the miracle cures, all the new curriculums and methods that at long last had arrived to rescue us from the depths of mediocrity. All the answers for low test scores, for low self-esteem, for apathy and indifference to learning.

Whatever happened to Values Clarification? Whatever happened to Career Education? Whatever happened to TESA, GESA, and the other ESA's? And what of the New Math? The New Science? Competency-based Education? Behavioral Objectives? The Hunter Model? Glasser Circles? And the list goes on. It may be difficult to imagine it now, but there was a time when each of the items we just listed was all the rage in educational circles. Some of them sank beneath the waves leaving no wake in their path. Others were forerunners of later trends and thus contributed to a certain extent to the ongoing search for better schools.

WHAT HAVE YOU DONE FOR US LATELY?

In an episode of "The Simpsons" cartoon show, Principal Skinner had hired young Bart Simpson to help him police the school. When all the Teacher's Guides turned up missing (stolen by Bart's own sister as it turns out), Bart suggested a schoolwide locker search. Principal Skinner suggested that such a procedure might be in violation of Supreme Court guidelines on students' Constitutional rights. Bart simply replied, rhetorically and convincingly, "What has the Supreme Court done for us lately?"

You might be posing a similar question as you read this book: "What have the Innovators done for us lately?" Well, as this book goes to press, the Restructuring Movement seems to be the wave of at least the near future. Look for School Restructuring, complete with site-based management, downsizing, schools-within-schools, interdisciplinary curricula, teacher empowerment, parent involvement, and real-world learning applications for students. This movement should persist for quite some time. It seems to us to be in many ways quite well founded. We have, in fact, been program evaluators for an award-winning Senior High School that is presently going through the throes of restructuring rather successfully. So, if we were asked "What is the dominant trend right now and for the foreseeable future?" we would say the Restructuring Movement.

Other things to look for that appear to have innovational promise include the Constructivist Movement, Computer and Related Technological Applications, and Cross-Age Teaming and Learning. We like the Constructivist Movement because it offers so much hope for active learning, personal involvement and ownership in knowledge. The idea that each of us constructs our own reality and that each of us interacts with knowledge slightly differently has the promise of freeing us from textbook-driven learning and the dreary seatwork that research tells us takes up so much of a child's schoolday.

We like the Computer Movement because it will lead the way to decentralizing libraries, providing Virtual Reality in learning, and freeing teachers to do the things that Piaget said teaching was really all about: Organizing, facilitating, and mediating the learning environment. The potential for technology to change the ways we learn and the ways we are able to gain access to knowledge appears to be unlimited. It's exciting just to imagine a young learner using computer technology to tap into the resources of the Library of Congress or using computer networks to find help with a mathematics problem.

We like the more natural grouping of people that occurs when schools break the traditional bonds of age-designated grades and levels. The idea that students should learn only with other students their own age is an idea whose time has come and gone. We look forward to a time when high school physics students explore simple machines and the accompanying principles of physics with elementary children. And we like the thought of young artists working with others beyond their age level in a cooperative spirit of creativity.

BEYOND EMPIRICISM

Much of the space in this book has been devoted to a look at the research base that supports certain educational innovations. It is our contention that teachers and administrators should demand evidence before plunging ahead into some effort that is sure to go away in time if for no other reason than that it never had a solid empirical basis. But this is not to say that every thing we do in the name of learning demands evidence based on carefully controlled studies. Some things that are done, or should be done, in the name of education are not of a nature to be empirically based.

Among the promising ideas that we assign to this category is increased parent involvement. Researcher John Goodlad has noted that where parents are aware and involved, school test scores are higher. We support his finding but know of no way that one could conduct a cause and effect experiment to determine the actual driving force in the mix of variables. But if we were building principals or classroom teachers we would do everything we could to get the parents meaningfully involved in the children's education. It not only is common sense, but it supports family togetherness.

Another example of something that we think does not need to wait for well-controlled research is the idea of apprenticeships in learning. School life, after all, unwittingly gave us the term "real world." Just imagine how motivating it would be for a high school student who dreams of a career in the health sciences field to get to spend several hours a week with professionals at a laboratory, clinic, or hospital. Apprenticeships bring a reality base to learning that we can't offer in the classroom. In that sense learning between real world and classroom complements each other.

We like the idea of portfolios in the assessment of learning process. Architects and artists have used them for years. We think portfolios empower students, allowing them to make decisions about what they feel is significant about their work. And we feel that keeping a portfolio helps a student to think about and be more aware of what he/she is learning along the way. If we were teaching in a classroom we would not wait for incontrovertible evidence that they raise test scores.

Another nonempirical school strategy is block scheduling. Block scheduling means getting away from the "one hour per day five days per week" mentality. In an art class, for example, it makes little sense to get out the paints, set up the easels, etc. and paint for a few minutes before it's time to clean everything up and put the equipment away. You don't need to paint every day, and you need more than a few minutes when you do paint. One could say much the same thing about a science lab experience or a discussion of values. The present schedule is a factory schedule, and it makes no sense in an information age.

Some of the other things that we would assign to this category include site-based management, staff development, mentoring, and greater use of the school facilities themselves. This grab bag of different things that teachers and administrators might consider could well be expanded.

One last prediction toward an improved learning environment in the schools that we will venture is the demise of the textbook as the dominant force in the curriculum. On the one hand, maybe we're just hoping it will happen. On the other hand, we think that if Restructuring, Constructivism, Technology, and Grouping fulfil their promises, textbooks as we know them won't be necessary.

RESEARCH QUESTIONS TO ASK

Anyone who contemplates significant educational innovation must ask three basis questions. Those questions have been at the heart of our own evaluations of the programs reviewed in this book. Those questions are:

1. What is the theoretical basis of the proposed program? And how sound is that theoretical base?

2. What is the nature of the research done to document the validity of the proposed program? How much and how good is the research done experimentally in classroom settings?

3. Is there evidence of large-scale implementation program evaluation? What comparisons were made with "traditional" forms? How realistic was the evaluation? What was the duration? What was the setting?

Our strong suggestion is that as you consider innovation, you pose these questions seriously. We think you should ask them of the purveyors of innovation. And we don't think you should settle for answers such as, "the movement is so new that much of this has not been done at this point." Too much is at stake.

A CLOSING THOUGHT

We've looked at a number of highly touted educational innovations in this book. In some instances we've been quite supportive. In others we've voiced serious reservations, especially where program evaluation studies are lacking. We certainly do not wish to make cynics out of our readers or to even suggest that you not consider an innovation until it has "proven" itself conclusively. If you waited for that, you would be, by definition, something less than an innovative school.

We are suggesting, however, caution, especially where large expenditures of funds are at stake. That is only prudent. But we do encourage risk taking, pilot programs, and efforts to transcend the ordinary qualities of school life. These efforts should be mounted as level 2 investigations. That alone will separate your school or district from the bandwagon hopping legions who merely think they are doing something innovative while actually practicing self-delusion. The other outcome of a commitment to level 2 research is that your school or district really will become a pilot center, one that others begin to look to for leadership. When schools commit to this level of quality, we can look forward to real progress, and perhaps the era of pendulum swings will come to a well-deserved end.

GLOSSARY

APPLIED RESEARCH — Research designs and applications to determine the effect of a given practice on specific educational outcomes. It is most often used to test a learning theory, or component of a learning theory, in actual or simulated classroom settings or learning situations, and conducted on a relatively small scale. For example, researchers may wish to determine the effect differing motivational strategies have on children's retention. To do so they may design an experimental study using the different motivational strategies in separate but relatively equivalent classrooms, looking for differential results on student retention. In this book, we have also referred to this type of research as **Level Two** research.

BASIC RESEARCH, also **PURE RESEARCH** — research on learning and behavior that is most commonly conducted in laboratory settings by psychologists, learning theorists, linguists, etc. Examples of this type of research would be medical research on brain functioning and behavioral research, such as operant and classical conditioning, by psychologists. The intent of this type of research is not to answer specific educational questions, but rather to serve as the basis for theories of how people learn and function. From this research are derived many learning theories with specific educational implications. It then becomes the job of the applied researcher to test the theories under controlled conditions to determine if they are valid. In this book, we have also referred to basic research as **Level One** research.

BRAIN-BASED TEACHING — Teaching approaches that are suggested by the theories derived from the basic research in brain functioning. The approaches generally require attention to hemisphericity, growth spurts, and modality. For example, a brain based teaching program might stress year-round schooling (growth spurts), curriculum integration (hemisphericity), and verbal and visual explanations (modality). It is theorized that such educational approaches will result in greater learning because of how the brain is thought to function.

CAREER EDUCATION — An educational movement which peaked during the 1970's. Basically, the career education movement attempted to incorporate career preparation into all aspects of the K-12 schooling system. The idea was that at all grades a student would be exposed to a wide range of career opportunities, with assistance in narrowing the choices based on the student's interests and aptitudes. In addition, career education was also intended to provide the student with the education and training appropriate for the career. Many states required teachers to take course work in career education, but movement is now in "the graveyard of lost ships."

CAUSE AND EFFECT — A concept in research where one variable is thought to effect a second variable is some measurable way. Cause and effect can only be theorized until it has been proven through experimental research. Basic research led to theories of cause and effect, but considerable applied research is necessary before it can be proven. Examples of cause and effect in education that have been generally proven by empirical research and accepted by the profession include reinforcement (cause) increases retention (effect) and mastery learning (cause) increases achievement (effect). Examples of cause and effect that have been theorized in education and that have *not* been proven by empirical research include modality teaching increases learning, style-based instruction increases learning, and thinking skills programs improve higher order thinking skills.

COGNITIVE DEVELOPMENT—A theory, or set of theories, which postulates that individuals pass through various and predetermined stages of intellectual functioning and abilities. Most notable of the theorists is Jean Piaget and Lawrence Kohlberg. Theses theories have considerable implications for how and when children should be taught various elements of the curriculum.

CONSTRUCTIVISM—A theory that learners construct their own knowledge and therefore their version of reality from their own unique experiences. It is this "construction" or schema that a learner then uses to accommodate and assimilate any new experience. The process of knowledge construction is thought to be an active one. Because of the complexities inherent in any real experience and because each learner's prior construction is unique, what someone learns in a given situation is often unpredictable.

COOPERATIVE LEARNING—An approach to the teaching/learning process which has been proposed as a viable alternative to the current individualistic and competitive practices of schools. There are several forms of cooperative learning, but they all involve students working in groups or teams to achieve certain educational goals. Its proponents propose it as a generic strategy that could be used in any setting, while others have designed subject-matter specific strategies. It is based on the theory of positive interdependence, with considerable **Level Two** research to support its use in the schools.

EMPIRICAL RESEARCH—A field of research in which knowledge is thought to be ascertained only through observation and experimentation. In empiricism, all proposed cause and effect relationships must be verified through experimental research.

It is the basis for the scientific method used in the "hard sciences." This methodology has been adopted by social science (and therefore educational) researchers and requires postulating a hypothesis and testing the hypothesis through data collection and analysis. While other forms of research may suggest cause and effect, only controlled experimental studies are accepted as "proof" of cause and effect. This type of research is sometimes called *quantitative* research because the data are generally reported in quantitative terms (test scores, frequency counts, etc.). Because quality experimental studies in education are extremely difficult to conduct, the empirical base for many innovations and new programs is very weak. In its absence many educators resort to qualitative research or anecdotal stories to show success.

ESSENTIALISM—An educational philosophy based on the belief that there is a core of essential knowledge and values that must be transmitted to students. Essentialists see the schools as a conserving, civilizing force in society. Essentialists curriculum represents a search for objective truth that can be known, and this results in emphasis on science, mathematics, language, and other basic skills subjects. Typically, subject matter is delivered through textbooks, and emphasis is placed upon testing, grading, objectives, outcomes, etc.

EVALUATION RESEARCH—Research designed to determine the efficacy of educational programs at the level of school of district implementation. Evaluation research is concerned with the effect of a large scale modification of an existing program or the implementation of a new program. Examples would be the evaluation of a staff development program in cooperative learning or the evaluation of a new mathematics curriculum in relation to student performance on standardized tests. Evaluation research may employ many of the same approaches as experimental research, it focuses on a different set of questions. Where experimental research is concerned with whether or not cooperative learning increases student achievement when it is used in the classroom, evaluation research is concerned with whether or not the programs can be successfully implemented on a large scale, and whether entire programs for schools or districts are actually successful if altering educational outcomes. In this book, we have also referred to this type of research as **Level Three** research.

EXISTENTIALISM – An educational philosophy based on the belief that the search for one's own sense of truth represents the purpose of and education. Freedom and personal choice are the keys to meaningful learning. Existentialists take issue with predetermined curricula as a guide to school learning. Rather the individual must determine what is important for him or herself. Such a decision might or might not take the form of formal schooling. A.S. Neill's Summerhill is a classic example of this school of thought.

EXPERIMENTAL RESEARCH – The most sophisticated of the empirical research designs and intended to show a cause and effect relationship between two variables. In its purest form, experimental research involves randomization and employs a control group with a differentiated treatment (cause) for the control and the experimental group. Measures are taken on a variable of interest (effect) usually before and after the treatment to determine the extent to which the treatment has effected the second variable. In education, pure experimental research is rare, leading to weak cause and effect conclusions. Many times the best that we can do is to use *quasi*-experimental research with intact groups, rather than random assignments.

FIELD DEPENDENCE/FIELD INDEPENDENCE, also **GLOBAL/ANALYTICAL** – A theoretical model proposed by Herman Witkin identifying two distinct ways in which people perceive stimuli. A field dependent/global person's perception is strongly influenced by the surrounding field, while the field independent/analytical person can perceive items apart from the surrounding field. This model of field perception has greatly influenced the learning styles movement and has resulted in a number of theories about personalities, teaching and learning.

GENERALIZABILITY — A concept in empirical research which addresses the degree to which an empirical finding for one group of people can be extended to a broader population. For example, if researchers have concluded from empirical research that students in California are deficient in math skills, can we therefore conclude that students in Florida are also deficient in math skills? If researchers have concluded that cooperative learning increases tests scores for 1st, 3rd, and 5th graders in a particular district, can we generalize those results to all elementary students in the district?

GROWTH SPURTS — Brain growth in children that medical research has shown happens in spurts, rather than in a continual and uninterrupted process. Based on the work of Herman Epstein, the research is often used to support the theories of cognitive development proposed by Jean Piaget. Growth spurts have suggested to educators various strategies such as individualized instruction and year-around school.

HAWTHORNE EFFECT — A situation in experimental research that can distort or alter the effects of the treatment, invalidating the experiment or, at a minimum, call the results into question. The Hawthorne effect is a situation in which the very act of conducting an experiment provides new or additional attention to the participants, thus altering their behavior and the experiment's outcome. An example would be an experiment where educators are interested in examining the effects of a teaching strategy. One group of teachers continues with the old methodology, while a second group of teachers is trained in the new method. Because this new method involves considerable attention given to these teachers, their attitudes and behaviors may change. Consequently, any increased learning on the part of the students may not be due to the new method, but rather to the attention the teachers received. In other words, it was not the method that produced the results, but the attention the teachers were given. Quality research projects consider the Hawthorne effect and control for it by various design features. Failure to do so makes the research results highly questionable.

HUNTER MODEL–A decisionmaking, instructional design model proposed by Madeline Hunter which gained prominence throughout the country during the 1970's and 1980's. There were claims of a strong research base to the model, but this meant very different things to different people. The model focused on four elements: Teaching to an objective; teaching at the correct level of difficulty; monitoring and adjusting instruction; and using the principles of learning. It served as the basis for extensive staff development activities, teaching evaluations, and was also extended to classroom management. There were scores of "trainers" across the country, with literally tens of thousands of teachers trained in the various procedures. The model had various names, including *Program for Effective Teaching (PET)* and *Instructional Theory Into Practice (ITIP)*.

INFORMATION PROCESSING – A theory that focuses specifically on the actual process of cognition. Attention is paid to a single act of learning at a particular time. For example, if we were to ask a child "How much is 5 times 3?" what factors would be involved in his/her "processing" of an answer? Information processing focuses on the process of learning rather than on the nature of the learner. Researcher Robert Sternberg of Yale has synthesized his ideas into a theory of intelligence which represents an attempt to quantify a learner's IP abilities. Sternberg has identified six information factors:

1. Spatial ability or the ability to visualize and solve problems through drawings, diagrams, maps or other spatial means.

2. Perceptual speed or the ability to grasp a perspective or new field of reasoning quickly.

3. Inductive reasoning or the ability to gather and sort evidence toward the making of inferences or the reaching of generalizations.

4. Verbal comprehension ability or the ability to understand new words, syntax, and ideas presented verbally quickly.

5. Memory or the ability to store and retrieve essential information.

6. Number ability or the ability to employ numerical reasoning and quantitative thought in problem solving.

INTEGRATION – *see* **INTERDISCIPLINARY STUDIES.**

INTERDISCIPLINARY STUDIES, also **INTERDISCIPLI-NARY CURRICULUM, INTEGRATION** – Terms used somewhat interchangeably to indicate the bringing together of separate disciplines around common themes, issues, or problems. Based in Progressive educational thought, interdisciplinary studies involve teacher teaming, students working together, real-world applications, and active, experiential learning.

ITIP, INSTRUCTIONAL THEORY INTO PRACTICE – *see* **HUNTER MODEL**

JOHN HENRY EFFECT – A situation in experimental research where the control group tries harder than normal because they know they are being compared against a "new" method of instruction or whatever. It is thought to be common in educational research when one methodology is being compared to another, because some teachers will work extra hard to show that the old method is as good as a new method. The result is inflated control group scores and invalid experimental results.

LANGUAGE ACQUISITION – A field of intellectual inquiry that focuses on the process by which children acquire language as they develop. The focus of the research is language acquisition as a "natural" occurrence, without direct instruction. How children acquire language is thought to have direct implications on how children should learn to read. The research on language acquisition serves as a component of the basic research for the whole language movement, with whole language advocates maintaining that reading should be a natural process of acquisition, much as language is acquired.

LANGUAGE EXPERIENCE – An approach to reading instruction of the 1970's which emphasized the importance of the child's own experience as a basis for learning to read and write. Instruction, therefore, focused on the student's experiences for reading and writing activities. Some educators have pointed to language experience as a forerunner to the current whole language movement.

LEARNING STYLES, also **COGNITIVE STYLES** – The consistent pattern of behaviors that can be associate with each individual as he/she approaches and interprets a learning experience. The basic research of this area is found in brain research and personality types. A number of models of learning styles have been proposed by individuals such as Rita and Kenneth Dunn, Marie Carbo, and Herman Witkin. Field dependent/field independent, abstract/concrete, and visual/ auditory/kinesthetic/tactile are just of a few of the styles which have purported to have been identified. Each of these styles have implications for how students should be taught, and each have strong advocates and inservice/training programs and materials available to schools.

LEVEL ONE RESEARCH – *see* **BASIC RESEARCH.**

LEVEL TWO RESEARCH – *see* **APPLIED RESEARCH**.

LEVEL THREE RESEARCH – *see* **EVALUATION RESEARCH**.

LONGITUDINAL RESEARCH – Research that is conducted over an extended period of time to study the long-term effects of a particular program. Longitudinal research is an important part of experimental and evaluation research and is used to determine if the effectiveness of a certain program declines or disappears over time. This is particularly important for eliminating the Hawthorne effect from educational research findings and strengthening conclusions regarding cause and effect.

MASTERY LEARNING – The instructional paradigm based on reductionism which postulates that given sufficient opportunity to learn and appropriate instruction, the vast majority of students can achieve some specified, expected level of achievement. Mastery learning generally involves the breaking down of any task, skill, or knowledge into its component parts and the mastery of those individual elements before moving on to the more difficult areas of learning. Mastery learning can be approached from an individualized instruction framework, or can be used in a large group situation, such as advocated by Benjamin Bloom. The general steps include identifying the appropriate learning objectives, teaching to those objectives, formative evaluation and feedback, reteaching when necessary, and summative evaluation.

MEANING CENTERED — An approach to learning which seeks relevance and avoids isolated skills as means of achieving literacy. Meaning centered instruction focuses on building knowledge and understanding within the natural framework of a child's experience, an important concept with the whole language educational philosophy.

METACOGNITION — A theory that states that learners benefit by thoughtfully and reflectively consideration the things they are learning and the ways in which they are learning them. A common phrase used by its advocates is "thinking about thinking." In classroom situations, metacognition could well involve "thinking aloud" with a partner, so that each participant gains insight to the processes that lead to intellectual conclusions.

MODALITY TEACHING — Using a variety of strategies, activities, explanations, etc. for the same content. Learning modalities are said to be sensory channels through which individuals give, receive, and store information. An outgrowth of brain research and learning styles, students are thought to be either visual, auditory, tactile-kinesthetic, or mixed modality learners. Modality teaching offers a variety of instructional approaches to reach the different types of learners. For example, modality teaching in arithmetic uses verbal explanations, written examples on the chalk board or on a handout, and manipulative hands-on math materials for the students which correspond to the task to be learned, thus employing multiple modalities and each helpful to the different types of learners.

MORAL DEVELOPMENT – A theory, or set of theories, which postulates that individuals pass through various and predetermined stages of moral reasoning. Most notable of the theorists is Lawrence Kohlberg. His theories were very influential during the 1960's and 1970's and resulted in a number of books, courses, and materials for teacher training in moral education and a wide number of moral education programs for children. These programs are currently in the "graveyard of lost ships."

MULTIPLE INTELLIGENCES – Howard Gardner's theory which attempts to broaden our definition of human intelligence. Gardner suggests that there are, in fact, seven forms of intelligence. they are:

1. Linguistic intelligence which involves sensitivity to the meaning of words, their order and syntax, the sounds, rhythms, and inflections of language, and the uses of languages.

2. Musical intelligence which consists of sensitivities to rhythm, pitch, and timbre. It also has an emotional component. Gardner relates musicians' descriptions of their abilities that emphasize an individual's natural feel for music and not the reasoning or linguistic components of musical ability.

3. Logical-mathematical intelligence which emerges from interaction with objects. By a sequence of stages the person is more able to perform actions on objects, understand the relations among actions, make statements about actions, and eventually see the relations among those statements.

4. Spatial intelligence which is the capacity to perceive the physical world accurately, to perform transformations and modifications on these perceptions, and to produce or recreate forms.

5. Bodily-kinesthetic intelligence which involves a person's ability to use the body in a highly specific and skilled ways, both for expressive (the dancer) and goal-directed (the athlete) purposes.

6, 7. Personal intelligence which takes two forms:
    a. Intrapersonal intelligence is the ability to access one's own feelings and to label, discriminate, and symbolically represent one's range of emotions in order to understand behavior.
    b. Interpersonal intelligence involves the ability to notice and make distinctions about other's moods, temperaments, motivations, and intentions.

NEW MATH – An approach to teaching mathematics during the 1960's and 1970's which was intended to revolutionize mathematics instruction. Its focus was to develop a conceptual understanding of the basic underlying principles of mathematics and problem solving, with less emphasis on the rote memorization of formulas. There is little evidence that the efforts were at all successful, and the New Math has been swallowed whole by the "back to basics" movement – another member of the "graveyard of lost ships."

OBE, OUTCOME BASED EDUCATION – An overall planning and restructuring process for schools or entire districts which proposes that desired educational outcomes should be the determining factor of the school calendar, administrative structure, and learning experiences. The design-down principle, a key concept in OBE, dictates that the curriculum and the resulting educational experiences should flow from the outcomes identified by the schools and communities, and not vice versa as is currently the general practice. Also central to OBE are the beliefs that all students can learn and succeed, not necessarily in the same way or at the same rate; success breeds success; and schools control the conditions of success. OBE is most closely associated with William Spady and is bolstered by "success stories" from around the country.

PART-TO-WHOLE LEARNING – The learning approach which is said to appeal to field independent/analytical learning styles. In part-to-whole learning, subject matter is taught and mastered in bits or components, and then synthesized into a whole entity. An example of part-to-whole learning would be the teaching of separate grammar rules and skills, and then asking a student to synthesize and employ them to write an essay – the inverse of whole-to-part learning.

PERENNIALISM – An educational philosophy based on the belief that there exists a set of absolute values (*e.g.*, justice wisdom, courage, etc.) that shape the curriculum. The source of these values is found in good literature, history mathematics, and science. For the perennialist, education is an end in itself because knowledge leads to virtue. Perennialists prefer original source material to textbooks, and they do allow for a range of teaching methods, *e.g.*, Socratic dialogue, seminars, investigations, etc. Mortimer Adler's *Paideia Proposal* is the best current example of perennialism.

PET, PROGRAM FOR EFFECTIVE TEACHING – *see*
HUNTER MODEL.

PHONICS – An approach to teaching reading which emphasizes individual letter and letter combination sounds as components of word formation. Phonics is closely associated with individual skills development, such as letter recognition, word attack skills, phonemes, digraphs, and blends. These skills are seen as prerequisites to the reading act, and that reading is the combination and use of these individually mastered skills. It is the "traditional" method of reading instruction and has been associated with basal reading programs.

PROGRESSIVISM – An educational philosophy which places emphasis on the growth and development of the individual child. They encourage active, spontaneous learning with a high degree of personal choice on the part of the learner. They downplay lessons plans, formal tests, graded curriculum, etc. Emphasis is placed on creativity and the arts. Progressives describe their form of teaching and learning as being directed at the whole child so as to create a balance among cognitive, affective, and physical learning.

QUALITATIVE RESEARCH – A research methodology that is largely subjective in nature, relying on observations, interviews, and interpretations of phenomena to provide information to the researcher. Other terms commonly used to describe the process are "ethnographic" and "naturalistic" research. Important aspects of qualitative research include: Research in a natural setting; human observation as the data gathering instrument; emphases on the social processes in the natural setting; and the use of intuitive insights. An example of the qualitative research process would be a researcher observing a classroom over an extended period of time describing and interpreting the activities, interactions, and processes of the classroom, coupled with interviews with the teacher and students on their perceptions of the efficacy of the classroom environment. Qualitative research has increased in the past twenty years, and it is slowly gaining acceptance in the profession.

QUANTITATIVE RESEARCH—*see* **EMPIRICAL RESEARCH**.

RECONSTRUCTIONISM—An educational philosophy based on the belief that the purpose of school is to build a better society. They place emphasis on group work, especially projects that have a "real world" focus. Reconstructionists view subject matter not as something you learn for its own sake, but as something you use as an empowering tool to create better conditions in society. Participatory citizenship is encouraged as opposed to an academic focus on separate subjects, letter grades, promotions, etc.

REDUCTIONISM, also **REDUCTIONIST APPROACH**—A theory of teaching and learning which maintains that all learning can be broken down into its constituent parts. This idea serves as the basis of behavioral objectives, lesson plans, and such evaluation measures as multiple choice, etc. The thinking is that by breaking whole entities into bits and pieces, the parts become more manageable and therefore more measurable.

RESEARCH BASED—A generic claim that implies there is a coherent empirical basis for the support and use of a particular theory or program being proposed by innovators or those seeking change. The term "research based" is readily misunderstood because three types of research bases may exist. The first type (Level One) is *basic* or *pure* research which can serve as the impetus for theories of learning. The second type (Level Two) is *applied* research which determines the effect of a given practice on specific educational outcomes. The third type (Level Three) is *evaluation* research which determines if the programs can be implemented successfully on a large scale and under what conditions. Before accepting claims that certain teaching strategies are research based, educators should demand quality research evidence at Level One and Level Two. Before accepting claims that new programs are research based, educators should also demand quality research evidence at Level Three.

RESTRUCTURING – A term that is currently in vogue which is a catch-all for a variety of reform efforts in schools. The term reflects the belief that American schools need drastic reformation in the most basic ways business is conducted. Current restructuring efforts in American schools generally involve some forms of teacher empowerment, site-based management, curriculum alignment/reform, choice, outcome-based education and/or community and parental involvement.

SOCIAL INTERDEPENDENCE, also **POSITIVE INTERDEPENDENCE**.

SPLIT BRAIN, also **HEMISPHERICITY** – A theory based on medical research which shows that the two hemispheres of the brain serve differing but complementary functions. The left hemisphere is associated with verbal, sequential, analytical abilities, while the right hemisphere is associated with global, holistic, visual-spatial abilities. These basic research findings on brain functioning are thought to have a number of implications for the classroom and have lead to a number of theories about teaching strategies appropriate for teaching to either hemisphere. To date, there is little applied research to support the theories.

STRUCTURE OF KNOWLEDGE – A theory which states that each discipline or body of knowledge has a basic structure composed of (1) its key ideas or concepts, and (2) its methods or process. For example, in anthropology "culture," "tradition," and "ritual" are concepts or key ideas and "participant observation," "interviews," and "qualitative assessment" are methods or processes.

TRIARCHIC THEORY OF INTELLIGENCE—Robert Sternberg's theory which suggests that intelligent human behavior consists of three components: (1) Thinking strategies or componential intelligence, including planning performance, and knowledge acquisition; (2) problem solving, or experiential intelligence, including insight, creativity, and efficiency; and (3) adaptation, or contextual intelligence, including selecting, reshaping, and maximizing.

VALUES CLARIFICATION—An educational approach in the 1970's which sought to help students understand their values and the values of others. The movement produced a number of books, courses, and materials for teacher training in values clarification and a wide number of values clarification programs for children. The movement lost steam by the end of the decade and was heavily criticized for its perceived relativistic view of values. These programs are currently in the "graveyard of lost ships."

WHOLE LANGUAGE—A philosophy of how literacy best develops in learners. In practice, whole language approaches have taken a variety of forms but with many common elements. It is a perspective on language and learning which is founded primarily on the use of literature programs, big books, predictable books, discussion groups, authentic stories rather than basal readers, acceptance of developmental spelling, and an emphasis on the writing process. Rooted in constructivist learning theory, meaning centered learning is a central tenet. Since language is the root of much of our learning, integration is seen as an important concept, with language experiences provided in all aspects of the curriculum. Natural learning situations and whole-to-part learning are also important whole language concepts. In a whole language environment the student is encouraged to learn to read and write much as he/she learned to speak, naturally. Intrinsic motivation and relevance are stressed as the teacher facilitates learning. Whole language instruction is being presented as an alternative to traditional basal reading programs which utilize extensive instruction in phonics and other isolated skills.

WHOLE-TO-PART LEARNING – The learning approach which is said to appeal to field dependent/global learning styles, and important in whole language philosophy. In whole-to-part learning, instruction begins with the "big picture," or in a natural setting. As the opportunity and need arises, students are helped to learn individual skills or content as they are needed in a particular setting and when they become meaningful. An example of whole-to-part learning would be asking students to write a story about something meaningful in their lives or within their realm of experiences. As students reread drafts of their stories, and as the needs arise, the stories can be edited and the various rules of grammar can be taught and used in a meaningful way – the inverse of part-to-whole learning.

INDEX